Come
Explore!

PERMISSION *SLIP

PERMISSION TO	DATE	SIGNATURE
* dream weave * your * reality *		CC.
Be your fucking soul Self!		CC
Run, Bambi, run!		CC

Permission Granted!

C.C. xo

That, over there. Yea, on the left. That's your Permission Slip – you never really needed one but now you have no excuse not to use it. This book will help you see all the ways you hold yourself back and all the shit that keeps you stuck. And this, this is your permission slip to move forward, to expand, or maybe to burn it all down and start over. I know, I know, it sounds cliché... but trust me, babe, we're gonna start clearing out whatever's holding you back and shift you into a higher state of creation.

'Okay, so what do I do now?'

You rip it out. *seriously!*

Yes, I want you to rip that page out of your *brand-new* book. *'Are you kidding me right now?'* No, babe, I'm not. Rip it out. Don't cut it or gently detach it – *rip it.* Use it as a bookmark, stick it on your fridge, your altar, your mirror, glue it to your fuckin' forehead for all I care, just tear it out. It doesn't matter how it looks – jagged edges, torn corners – that's the point. Break the rules, act a lil' weird, fuck around and find out. Do you remember what it feels like to be a messy, playful little rascal? I do. And it's fun over here, babe. So, come on in – the water's nice.

Now, I've taken the liberty of permitting you to do a couple things already, but the rest is for you to fill out as you explore this book. We're going to experiment with shifting your perspective, your energy, your future, your past (yes, shifting your past – but don't worry, we'll explore bending time and activating abundance later). For now, I welcome you to your first experiment: Tear that shit out. When you do it, notice how you feel. Liberated? Guilty? A little stressed? *'My brand-new book!'* I feel so naughty telling you to do this. I love it. For the troublemakers at heart this might feel easy. For the perfectionists, people pleasers, overachievers, good students, micromanagers, approval seekers, and those alike, you might feel on edge. Perfect. Let's walk the edge of your current reality and see what's beyond it.

Ready? Great! Now rip that Fucker right out.

Ready? I am. Deep breath. Go ahead, commit your little book crime. Then ask yourself: *How did that feel?*

Welcome to The Audacity Experiment.

K, Seriously...
Go back and rip
that fucker out!

The Audacity Experiment ☺ ♡
xo

The Audacity Experiment ☺♡
xo
Chris Corsini

HAY HOUSE

Carlsbad, California • New York City
London • Sydney • New Delhi

C.C. xo

Published in the United Kingdom by:
Hay House UK Ltd, 1st Floor, Crawford Corner,
91–93 Baker Street, London W1U 6QQ
Tel: +44 (0)20 3927 7290; www.hayhouse.co.uk

The information given in this book should not be treated as a substitute for professional medical advice; always consult a medical practitioner. Any use of information in this book is at the reader's discretion and risk. Neither the author nor the publisher can be held responsible for any loss, claim or damage arising out of the use, or misuse, of the suggestions made, the failure to take medical advice or for any material on third-party websites.

The QR codes included in this book link to external content created and maintained solely by the author, Chris Corsini. Hay House UK Ltd. is not responsible for the availability, accuracy, or ongoing maintenance of these external resources.

A catalogue record for this book is available from the British Library.

Hardcover ISBN: 978-1-83782-594-3
E-book ISBN: 978-1-83782-595-0
Audiobook ISBN: 978-1-83782-596-7

10 9 8 7 6 5 4 3 2 1

This product uses responsibly sourced papers, including recycled materials and materials from other controlled sources. For more information, see www.hayhouse.co.uk

The authorized representative in the EU for product safety and compliance is Penguin Random House Ireland, Morrison Chambers, 32 Nassau Street, Dublin D02 YH68, Ireland. https://eu-contact.penguin.ie

Printed and bound by CPI Group (UK) Ltd, Croydon CR0 4YY.

Dedications

I dedicate this book to my many teachers, both seen and unseen, and to all those who walk beside me, in-person and behind the veil.

And to my greatest friend, Don. What you so generously gifted me, at a time when I needed it most, has blossomed into something that reaches far beyond anything we could have ever imagined. I only hope the encouragement, wisdom, love, and acceptance you poured into me spills out in every direction, to each end of this beautiful Earth, and reaches those who need it now.

I dedicate this book to my fellow seekers; may the light that guides you never dim, even in the darkest of nights.

I dedicate this book to my future self – thank you for liberating me with every step toward you.

Lastly, I dedicate this book to Christopher Paulie. Please remember, you were always enough.

I love you.

Contents

START HERE **xiii**
Introduction xv
A Few Ways to Use This Book xxi
What's Alive for You xxxi

PART 1: THE AUDACITY TO QUESTION EVERYTHING **1**
The Self vs. The Soul 5
Who Are You Now, Why, and How? 8
You're Programmed 12
Microchips 16
Lose Your Fucking Mind ← I did & you can too! 18
Judgment 20
People Are Trees 23
Bending Time 25
Try Something New 29

PART 2: THE AUDACITY TO FEEL IT ALL **31**
insanely helpful
Your Body Is Technology 35
Nervous System 101 40
Pause with the Panic 44
Alchemize Energy 49
Emotions: What Are they? 52
WTF Am I Feeling and Why? 58
Your Magnetic Mind 60
Pivot the Pattern 64
Triggers and Flags (Pain Points) 71

← life Changing

} How to actually manifest your dream life

Handwritten annotations: Spoiler: Balance isn't real! · love this part. · $$ $

How Exciting!

START HERE

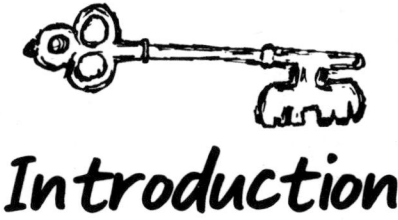

Introduction

I didn't plan to write a book – but here we are. **lol**

If you looked up Chris Corsini five years ago, you wouldn't have found him. I was working as a bartender – slanging beers and scarfing down cold chicken fingers dipped in hot honey with my best friend Dani in the back room. It was fun. It wasn't always easy, but it was safe. It wasn't fully aligned. It wasn't entirely me. It honestly wasn't all that audacious, but it was something... and honestly, I needed the money.

What really excited me was tarot, astrology, and working with my intuitive gifts. At that time, I began to realize I was like an X-Man as all this weird shit had started happening. I'd studied with an incredible mentor and would do different types of psychic readings for people here and there, but I couldn't imagine making a living from it (and neither could my mom). Then little by little, things started shifting. I leaned into doing more of what I loved: tarot, workshops, astrology, creating community gatherings, and doing the deep energetic work that actually moves people. I dove deeper into the magic behind everything and started to see the hidden layers of the world around us. So, down the rabbit hole I went. I followed the flow, and let me tell you, the flow seriously took me places. It led me to Europe and eventually landed me in Portugal. I explored retreats in the woods, I purged, I expanded, I had ceremonies that cracked me open, I hosted online circles with thousands of you tuning in from around the world.

find your flow.

My online presence exploded into millions of people following my work. And eventually, this book happened. How's that for flow?

I could have never imagined what we were creating. All of us – you reading this, the people who show up to my workshops, the random lady who asked me if I wanted to write a book (thanks, Amy!), and the team who helped bring this book to life. We actually built something. A weird, powerful, playful, expansive thing, and now it's yours, too. So, I hope you like it, because it took me 36 years of trials and tribulations to figure this shit out, and we're just scratching the surface.

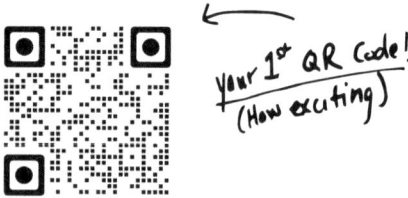

So, WTF is The Audacity Experiment?

It's not a system. It's not a five-step plan. It's not me pretending I have it all figured out. (Spoiler: I don't.) It's an invitation to try something different. To live differently. To think differently. To experiment with your energy, your story, your reactions, your rituals, your relationships. To ask yourself: *What happens when I stop performing and start being real? What if I stop trying to fix myself – and start trusting who I've been all along? What if I already have everything I need to pivot, to let go, to create the life I always dreamed of? What if I deserve more, and what if I can actually get it?*

That's what audacity means to me. Choosing yourself over the bullshit we've been told to buy into. It's choosing your truth over your conditioning. It's the boldness to be seen as a weirdo and not care what other people think. The willingness to fuck it up and try again. Audacity means doing the thing that's true to you even when your voice shakes, or your inner critic screams, or your parents won't approve. It's not about perfection. It's about presence. It's about being who you really are, underneath the bullshit of who you thought you needed to be. The audacity to be you.

Trust me when I say this: I do *not* have the perfect life. I don't float around all day in white linen drinking ceremonial cacao and humming mantras while my chakras sparkle. I once had this transcendent channeling session where energetic wisdom keepers showed me these insane light codes and I was, like, dancing with Shiva in ceremony. Literally hours later, I was on my hands and knees scrubbing diarrhea off my Moroccan rug because my dog shit himself while I was out. Transcendence. Then dog shit. All in one day. Both are real. Both are sacred. That's showbiz, baby.

This is not about creating the ideal life, because it doesn't exist. But we can create an incredible life we love. This book is full of reflections, insights, rituals, and tools that have helped me on my journey. But also: mistakes. Chaos. Laughter. Some things will resonate. Some won't. That's fine. It's not one-size-fits-all. Think of it like a spiritual snack pack: Taste what you want, spit out what's not for you, and come back for seconds when you're hungry. There's no test. No right or wrong. No 'doing it perfectly.'

Throughout this book you'll find QR Codes *(see page xxx)* – these pixelated little squares that might look like static on your television screen but actually act as a secret portal; yes, they're a living link that will re-route you into a digital world designed to support you on your journey. Each scan will take you beyond the page, offering free tools, practices, and conversations that you can experiment with and integrate into your life as you see fit. You'll discover conversations with some of my favorite thought leaders from diverse communities, and get some behind-the-scenes glimpses into the breakdowns and breakthroughs I had while writing this book. This digital world we're creating is not just where you'll find a whole new community to journey with through this book and beyond; it's

important!

also a living, breathing entity of its own where we'll update and rotate the speakers, practices, and offerings — so as you evolve, so does this book. This way, we can walk side by side as we grow together. This book is like your key, the QR codes are the portal, and the places we bring you might just be the guidance you need for your next chapter.

A juicy lil' surprise!

We'll always include free resources to help you, first and foremost. If you're interested in diving even deeper, you'll see where you can donate or contribute to supporting the teachers, speakers, practitioners, and their communities alike. The extended programs and offerings are resources intentionally priced to stay highly accessible, and every contribution becomes part of a larger cycle of support. Proceeds directly support the individuals you'll meet here, allowing them to continue doing this work. A portion flows back to their communities through charities, programs, and initiatives that provide an arrangement of things, including but not limited to clean water, education, accessibility, employment opportunities, creative expression, and the amplification of marginalized voices. In this way, choosing to invest in your deeper learning is not only a gift to your own growth but a ripple that creates support and change for others. We are in this together, babe. Thank you for being here.

I want to be honest with you from the jump: I'm not special. I mean, I *am* — and so are you — but nothing presented in this book, or elsewhere, is meant to place me above you. I'm not ahead of you. If anything, I'm a little deeper into the mess, shouting back that the water's fine.

I've been that kid dry-heaving in turmoil in the high school bathroom. I've been that quiet loner eating lunch outside behind the garbage bins with my only friend Jenna because at times we couldn't handle being visible. And now? I do work that's deeply meaningful to me, strangers come up to me in the street to tell me how much I've helped them, and I randomly get fun invitations to private parties on superyachts to read tarot for A-list celebrities. The pendulum swings both ways!

But you don't get to create a life you love if you're not willing to look at the stuff that had you dry-heaving on the bathroom floor in the first place. One of the things that has been transformative for me is an understanding of how to work with different energies. Even if I don't always use the knowledge I have, or apply it every single day of my life, I think it's worth sharing, which is exactly what I'm doing here. It's brought me a lot of peace. It's brought me a lot of inspiration. It's brought me a lot of tears, and it's brought a lot of mirrors reflecting back the changes required. It's also brought me a lot of joy, a shit ton of money, and plenty of opportunities to play. My life is still a mess in some ways, but it's a beautiful mess that I can laugh my way through, while trusting the flow and readjusting when needed.

This book isn't about having a breakthrough and living happily ever after. It's about learning to live through the in-between. It's about becoming the kind of person who can understand their own energy – and shift it. Who can feel their feelings, meet their shadow, move their body, and get back in alignment. Who can laugh at the mess and trust the magic.

You might not be there yet. That's totally fine. This is your permission slip to begin. We're not aiming for perfection. We're aiming for purpose. You just have to *show up*.

So, take what works. Adjust it. Apply it. Fuck it up. Learn. Start again.

The life you've created is the one you're in. The life you want is the one you can create.

That's the experiment. That's the audacity. That's the invitation.

Now let's begin.

I tried something different here...

A Few Ways to Use This Book

I get it — you don't need to be told how to read a book! But bear with me. I'm not trying to reinvent the wheel, but I do want you to start thinking differently, and that starts with shaking up your preconceptions.

You Lead the Way   _Classic!_

Choose your own adventure. You can read through the book in a traditional way; there's a nice cohesive flow from start to finish if you prefer a straight read through. Or get a lil' silly and jump around — open random pages or select a piece that feels right. You'll find suggested readings in some pieces, too. Like leapfrog, you can jump from lesson to lesson, as you wish, and dabble in the QR Codes along the way.

Seasons of Life (emotional)

Just like nature, we, too, move through our own seasons. We are not separate from nature, or these cycles. We are not always blooming like in a moment of summer. Things change. We flow through phases of release, creation, expansion, and decay. Our internal cycles and personal seasons do not always match the natural seasons. We can still look at them to better understand ourselves and what we may be moving through. As I'm sure you know, some days we might swing through a few seasons, feeling great in the morning, excited as spring, and by the evening, needing deep rest and recovery, like winter. Some days we feel bold AF, other days we need to hibernate alone with Netflix and pizza. The Seasons of Life helps you understand what energies you're moving through on any given day and provides suggested readings that align with those moments.

There are a few ways to engage with this approach. One, read through the description of the seasons and identify which one you feel most aligned with, then dive into a suggested reading. If you're like, 'I have no fucking clue what season I'm in right now.' Cool, then you can fill out the Seasonal Sorting Quiz *(see page xxvi)* and I'll help you figure it out. Once we identify your season, dive into one of the suggested readings. The last approach is to use the Wordsearch – intuitively find a word, and that word will lead you to a season. Then, you guessed it, dive into one of the suggested readings.

If you like the first approach, you can find The Seasons below with their full descriptions, some key words that might resonate with you, and their suggested readings.

Spring – An Invitation for Renewal and Awakening

This is a moment of change, but it can feel like an upswing into something exciting. Maybe you're feeling playful or eager for what's to come. This is an energy of curiosity and intrigue. A moment for you to feel into all the possibilities before you – like there's a bunch of doors in front of you, and you kinda wanna kick one open and jump right TF in. You may feel surprisingly vulnerable, or maybe you have butterflies and feel like you're gonna shit yourself, but either way this is where a new journey begins!

KEY WORDS: hopeful, curious, tender, restless, impatient, alive, ready, inspired, eager, uncertain, tingly with excitement

This is a season for planting seeds, but keep in mind that sometimes it's nice to balance things out with the opposite, so if none of these chapters feel interesting, maybe you need to explore some of the opposing fall energy. If you're feeling overly impatient, maybe take a peek at winter for stillness or release.

Summer – Feeling Excited, Expansive, and Expressive

This is a moment of bold, straightforward energy. It can feel like things are lining up in your favor, or maybe a couple things are in bloom but they're actually weeds and it's time to trim the fat. Either way, you may feel creative or confident about taking action. There's a lot of outward energy. Emotions can be amplified – your highs can be expansive and your lows can feel like burnout. Summer brings with it realizations (kinda like the Full Moon), and not necessarily ones you're happy about. I find that when everything is in bloom it's a great time to take inventory – what's working in my life? What isn't? What can I actually do about it?

KEY WORDS: expressive, colorful, proud, aware, creative, generous, carefree, passionate, abundant, radiant, feels like you're holding a lot, under pressure, overexposed

Summer is a season of culmination; you're likely gaining awareness around what needs to happen next. If these chapters don't immediately appeal, it may interest you to balance out your summer vibes with the opposite energy – look toward winter for rest or release. If you still haven't found what you're in need of, search fall for reflection.

Fall – A Moment of Harvest and Release

Fall is about letting go – the leaves are changing and true colors are being revealed. This is a moment to recognize what your investments have brought; your time, energy, money, love, attention. What did you get in return for your commitments? What's nourishing you? What's depleting you and needs to go? The fall season reminds us that nothing lasts forever, and it brings an opportunity to prepare space for something new. Maybe you're ready to let go of an outdated habit or relationship. Maybe you're feeling grateful for your hard work paying off and entering a moment of stability. Whatever it is, the moments of fall are inviting us to see things differently.

KEY WORDS: change, integration, gratitude, reflective, surrender, cautious, wise, acceptance, nostalgic, sadness, completion, initiation, release, grief

SUGGESTED CHAPTERS: Bending Time *(see page 25)*; Triggers and Flags (Pain Points) *(see page 71)*; Disappointment (ft. Ariana Grande) *(see page 78)*; Cutting Cords *(see page 122)*; Integration *(see page 125)*; Self-Sacrificing and People Pleasing *(see page 136)*; People and Projections *(see page 159)*; Purpose and Priorities *(see page 230)*

This is a season of pivoting toward something new. You can feel that change is in the air as your emotions turn inward inviting you to investigate where you're at. What are you ready to leave behind? What are you currently passing through? If the suggested chapters don't resonate you may feel called to balance things out with the opposite energies – look toward spring for a sense of renewal, or lean into summer for lightness and joy if you feel like you're taking things too seriously.

Winter – Required Stillness and Fertility

Winter is always an interesting season. In nature, we're surrounded by death and decay, and we often find ourselves in a bit of a slump. It's not a time to force expansion. It's not a time to push yourself; it's a time for rest and recovery. You're actually more productive when you gift yourself time to be less productive. Don't confuse speed with progress. The energy of winter provides us with the decomposition required to create the fertile soil needed for our next cycle. It's not weak to slow down, it's wise. This is a season of wisdom, of listening to that inner voice asking you to pause. Winter brings with it a womb for creation; a calling we so often ignore. This is a season of deep rest, healing, and inner vision. Surrender and have patience. It's a journey into the underworld to reflect on and understand where we've come from and how we've created certain things. It helps us untangle and unburden ourselves so we can expand in seasons to come.

KEY WORDS: quiet, still, lonely, contemplative, restorative, suffering, grief, surrender, trust, allowance, acceptance, dissolving, calling back your energy, reclamation, refueling

SUGGESTED CHAPTERS: Pause with the Panic *(see page 44)*; Shadow Work *(see page 87)*; Tell Them You Love Them *(see page 92)*; Stuck *(see page 96)*; Shame *(see page 107)*; Grief and Releasing *(see page 110)*; Energetic Boundaries *(see page 175)*; The Audacity to Be Soft Yet Bold *(see page 252)*

Winter invites gestation. A moment for us to incubate and regenerate our body, liberate our mind, and anchor deeper into our soul. This is a moment of deep nourishment and alchemy. Experiment with slowing down and taking more time for yourself. If things are feeling particularly dense, or stagnation is building too much, possibly explore the energies of summer to rebalance. Summer can bring movement and action. If you feel too isolated or a need to lean into fresh ideas to shake things up, perhaps explore the suggested chapters of spring. Don't avoid winter though; it's here to nourish us deeply and provides significant and required change for the better. Explore the winter chapters; but don't lose yourself in the darkness that sometimes accompanies those cold, dark nights. These are perfect moments to connect with community and lean on those you can. We're all in this together. Find our online community on page 143. You're not alone.

Seasonal Sorting Quiz

If you can't quite tell which energetic season you're vibing in right now from these descriptions, take this quiz. Read each of the following 10 statements and give them a number from 1 to 5 based on whether you strongly agree (5), agree (4), feel neutral (3), disagree (2) or strongly disagree (1). Don't overthink it; just go with your gut.

Grab your fancy-pants journal, your Notes app, or the back of an old receipt – whatever works – and keep a running tally as you go. We're not aiming for perfection here, just a little energetic self-awareness.

1. Physically, I have energy and I can get shit done!   1 2 3 4 5

2. My mind is clear, sharp, and at peace.   1 2 3 4 5

3. I'm open and curious to new ideas, experiences, and suggestions.   1 2 3 4 5

4. Emotionally, I feel stable and solid.   1 2 3 4 5

5. I'm motivated and passionate about things in my life right now.   1 2 3 4 5

Strongly disagree!

Strongly Agree!

6. My sense of purpose and direction feels clear. 1 2 3 4 5

7. I could totally take a risk. I'm cool with change
   and the unknown. 1 2 3 4 5

8. I feel connected to myself, my body, and who I am. 1 2 3 4 5

9. I feel expressive and inspired. I wanna
   create something! 1 2 3 4 5

10. I feel in flow with life, supported by the Universe,
    and at ease. 1 2 3 4 5

Now add up your total – circle it, star it, highlight it in neon pink, whatever your little heart desires – and then match your score to the Seasonal Key:

10–19: Winter

20–29: Fall

which Season
are you in?

30–39: Spring

40–50: Summer

Come back to this quiz whenever you need a vibe check on where you're at. You'll be shocked (or not) by how often your season shifts. That's the whole point: you're an evolving creature. Let the seasons be your guide.

Intuitive Wordsearch *My Fave!*

If you're drawn to play and spontaneity, try the Intuitive Wordsearch. Scan the page, let your eyes land on a word that resonates, and trust it. That word will connect with a season in the key. Then read the relevant description on pages xxii–xxv – feel free to choose any of the suggested readings that fall under the season you've found yourself in, there's likely something there you need to hear.

Intuitive Wordsearch

```
D P B L U R L J X R M Q M J M
Z U T R H O P X C A C H E H S
P A Y U E R E C E I V E N L L
W R E S T A J K W V E U U E H
I W B K X Q K Y F A I T E A M
U Q E N L B U J L P J F Q D T
P E L P B Y G E D O R A V C T
L Y I V H V T C S L K S E P E
A Y E I Y T C L R T S N F W E
Y B V L Y V Y L U E N X L I X
Q E E W E H H E E O A O A T P
H J H J P X V W C A X T N C A
D L V R E L E A S E N R E N N
S C Z V T R E N E W T S X U D
T I A D J U S T B U R I E T C
M K O F Y S Q R Z L A D H P N
E J U V C M T B X Y R O I S V
A L Q N F P H E K J M C U Z Y
```

★ Found a word?
Great! ⤳ →

Intuitive Wordsearch Key

- RENEW – Spring (*see page xxii*)

- RECEIVE – Fall (*see page xxiv*)

- CONNECT – Summer (*see page xxiii*)

- RELEASE – Fall (*see page xxiv*)

- BREAK – Fall (*see page xxiv*)

- REST – Winter (*see page xxv*)

- QUESTION – Winter (*see page xxv*)

- BELIEVE – Spring (*see page xxii*)

- CREATE – Summer (*see page xxiii*)

- PLAY – Summer (*see page xxiii*)

- FEEL – Winter (*see page xxv*)

- ADJUST – Fall (*see page xxiv*)

- EXPAND – Spring (*see page xxii*)

- CLEANSE – Spring (*see page xxii*)

- ACHE – Winter (*see page xxv*)

These are the seasons tied to each word ☺

Please remember, like everything else in life, these seasons come and go. *This too shall pass.* I know it's clichéd AF but it's true. This is one of the many ways to explore and experiment with this book, and depending on where you're at right now, it might be the best. If you're not excited about navigating the book this way, great! I'm so glad I just spent two hours designing it.

Experiment

Over time, try exploring this book in different ways. There's no right or wrong way to do it. Move through it intuitively, seasonally, or just open a random page and start there. Read the book from cover to cover, or quiz yourself and make your choice based on a daily (or hourly) check-in. I trust in your ability to navigate this journey, and so should you. Choose your own adventure. This is meant to be playful, not instructional. Have at it.

Don't Forget the QR Codes

Throughout this book, you'll find QR codes that link to extra practices, discussions, and resources *(see page xviii)*. All of these resources can also be accessed via www.theaudacityexperiment.com. Over time, these resources will be updated so there's fresh support for you to tap into. These resources allow you to experiment, grow, and evolve beyond the pages of this book, so don't skip them!

These are insanely supportive!

☆ ASL Edition

Yes, we went there. *The Audacity Experiment* is also available in an American Sign Language edition, because accessibility matters and everyone deserves access to this work. If ASL is your preferred language, or part of how you experience the world, you'll find a fully signed version waiting for you. Turn to page 266 for more details, including the QR code.

What's Alive for You ?

We've all got shit to work through. Good shit, bad shit – it's all there. I could write about my unhealthy patterns till the cows come home – and trust me, you'll hear about 'em – but in these pages and through these practices, you'll confront your own shit. I'll help you clear some of it out so you can build something more authentic, anyway.

So... where do you even start? How do you know what needs to change? Sometimes it's insanely obvious, sometimes it's a gentle whisper that we pretend to ignore. When you experiment with this book, you'll start to notice what changes are needed to find more freedom. You'll find hidden magic in different opportunities. You'll begin to expand.

I asked over 10,000 people what frustrates the hell out of them, where they feel they're stuck, how they wish to expand, and what friction they continue to rub up against. These are some of the things they wanted guidance on:

- Finding better flow in life

- Letting go of people, stories, and old feelings

- Setting boundaries without aggression

- Understanding the houses in your birth chart and what each planet means

- Standing in your power and not catastrophizing

- Making great money doing work that brings you joy and fulfillment

- Cleaning and protecting your energy from people who make you feel uncomfortable

- Discovering your purpose when you feel lost

- Reconnecting to creativity, motivation, and joy

- Healing scarcity and trusting divine timing

- Getting clarity around desires and direction

- Finding love, connection, and community

Common threads showed up again and again: intuition, letting go, reclaiming power, finding purpose, making money, setting boundaries, trusting the process, manifesting your dream life without bypassing the bullshit.

One of the loudest themes? Letting go. It makes sense, we can't expand into a new life with new opportunities, if we're still holding onto the past. That's why I've dedicated a whole section of this book to it: Part 3: The Audacity to Let Go. In it, you'll find a full chapter on Cutting Cords *(see page 122)*. This isn't just about releasing your toxic ex or overbearing parent. It's about letting go of outdated versions of yourself too – the fears, the habits, the agreements you never really meant to make. All of that can be shifted, clearing space for so much more. And honestly, it *should* be shifted. So, let's shift that shit.

Your Starting Point

Now it's your turn. Look back at the list. Do any specific themes resonate? Feel free to circle two or three that stand out. Don't overthink it – just notice what pulls at you. Those are your starting points. Those are what's most alive for you, for now.

And here's the thing: You're not alone. We're all carrying the same shit in a different backpack. Different flavors, same menu. The details change, but the path is more similar than not. There's something comforting about knowing that – like, yeah, you're a unique little weirdo, but you're also part of a whole community of cute lil' weirdos. We're all talented, and we're all just as confused as you are, babe. We're all just trying our best to figure it out. And as Ram Dass once said, we're all just walking each other home.

Stop thinking you need to fix everything. Just start where you're at.

It's time to play. Welcome to the work.

let's begin!

THE AUDACITY TO ?

Question <u>Everything</u>

(PART ONE)

Okay, let's get weird. This section of the book is intended to give you a chance to press pause and ask yourself the big questions: Who am I, really? What makes me the way I am?

How did I end up here, in this exact moment of my life?

Think of it like a living experiment: The Hypothesis of Who I Am. *A hypothesis is just a working theory, right? And that's basically all your identity is – a bundle of stories, labels, and characters you've been dragging around. 'I'm Chris.' 'I'm an astrologer.' 'I'm a brother, a son, a Canadian living in Portugal, apparently an author now (who let that happen?).' We're all wrapped up in a cute little package. But are we actually any of those things? Are we only those things? No. Not really. They're experiences. Roles. Masks. And they shift over time.*

Who I was 10 years ago isn't who I am today, and who I think I am right now is only a theory based on my past and the meaning I give to it. Or the stories I tell myself about my past experiences. What if I'm actually none of those things?

So, what if we start testing those theories? What if we tug on the threads of the stories we've inherited, the characters we've been playing, the behaviors that never really belonged to us in the first place? And what if it all unravels?

Good. That's the point. Because once it unravels, you get to write the story yourself. You get to reshape and realign with what you truly want – not what your parents, teachers, religion, culture, or Instagram algorithm told you to want.

This part of the book is about noticing the scripts you've been running on autopilot, questioning them, and experimenting with new ways of thinking, feeling, and showing up. It's about loosening the grip of your old ways, or your conditioning, so you can create the space to choose differently.

We can replace the unconscious 'I am who I was told to be' with a conscious choice. To be who we want. To be who we truly are. Let's question it all.

Soul

Self

The Self vs. The Soul

We all have a soul, our unique essence. It's the wildly expressive, untamed parts of ourselves that help us find fun, flow, and creation. It connects us to the Universe, or God, or Source, or whatever you believe in. It's the real you, deep down, under all the bullshit. And then there is the 'self' – the way we construct ourselves and everything that is conditioned by our stories, belief systems, family relationships, our upbringing, society, and other external forces. A part of this is our ego, the summation of the stories passed on through generations and genetics, the moments, identifiers, roles, and experiences that have created a construct of who the 'I' is in how we choose to identify ourselves and navigate the world around us. The ego isn't inherently bad, it helps us understand who we are in this world. It's necessary and supportive when aligned with the soul, but when the ego (the self) is misaligned and in total control, then, Houston, we have a problem.

The self helps us orient who we are in relation to space and time. There are many layers that create the entirety of who we are, how we are, and what we do. Some of these invisible layers include our ethereal and energetic body, our mental body, our emotional body, our spiritual self, and our egoic self. All of this lands in the densest form of all, our physical body *(see more on this in Your Magnetic Mind on page 60)*. This is why it's so important to move the energies on all layers and not just focus on one. A change in one layer ripples out into all the others. And our physical body is an insanely powerful tool to help us understand what's happening on all other layers.

The self, including the body, is a bit of a wild beast. It can be trained and conditioned into certain ways of behaving, it can be tricked into certain ways of thinking, and it can find immense safety in the predictability and comforts of routines and connections (even if they're not benefitting you). It can become rife with fears and anxieties. It can reach for coffee, wine, cigarettes, a bigger house, more followers online. The self is full of unconscious addictions, imposed belief systems, limitations, tendencies and habits that aren't always serving us. It responds well to praise and tries to avoid pain. It needs maintenance and repair. It has to be charged back up with eating and sleeping. Over time the self, that is the mind connected to the body, finds the things it likes and it sticks with it. The self is shaped through our experience and the meaning we attach to those experiences. It is made up of our mindset, our choices, and our stories – this becomes our avatar – how we move through life and all that we do.

you can retrain the body

The self can be a pain in the ass. It can keep us trapped in what we think we want and who we think we are. It can be tempted and teased, it can be controlled and controlling. A real piece of work. But we can liberate ourselves from the selves that don't serve us to deeper align our self with our soul. Both the self and the soul share one body, a beautiful body with all its aches and pains, the butterflies in the stomach, the miserable shakiness before having to give a speech. It gives us information; a constant stream of data that helps us understand what's really going on, where we're aligned, or not, but only if we pay attention. Our body, physically, has amazing technology that can help us align the self and the soul (see Your Body Is Technology on page 35). The body helps us move stuck energy from the past, anchor into the present, and co-create our future.

We're always either in a dance with, or a battle between, our soul and our self. We're in disarray, depression, friction, or frustration, or we find expansion, expression, liberation, and flow. Coherence is when both the self and soul are aligned.

The soul is soft.

The soul loves to grow, to expand.

The soul likes nothing better than entering a state of discovery and play. ♥ (inner child)

When you let yourself access it, you will feel a gentleness descend over you. A sense of peace. No struggling, no panic about *what has to be done right fucking now*. Your soul is patient; it's always okay right where it is. The soul does not rush. The soul is the tortoise, not the hare.

To unlock our greatest potential we need to find coherence between the body, the self, and the soul. How else could you receive your greatest blessings if not by being your truest self?

When the self and the soul are in alignment, this is where magic happens. This is how miracles happen. This is where we find our flow. This kicks open the doors to opportunities, abundance, health, freedom, and everything else we desire. Because when we're vibrating at a frequency of true authenticity, the Universe shows up like never before.

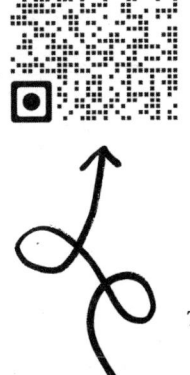

Who Are You Now, Why, and How?

Take a look around.

You are living the 3D consequential result of where your attention, actions, and energy have been. This is why I work specifically with the New/Full Moon six-month cycles because they give you an anchor to work with. If you focus your energy and actions into something for six months, the exact time it takes for a New Moon in Leo to become a Full Moon in Leo, for example, you will see the culmination and results of commitment, whether it be a few steps forward, or a massive leap. You built everything that got you to this moment. You're already co-creating your reality. Most people don't even realize they're already using the tools I share throughout this book. I want to help you pull back the curtain and better understand these tools so you can build your life intentionally, and not from someone else's blueprint. Many of the directions you received and the pathways you walked came from a source that was trying to extract something from you. A force trying to use your labor, your creativity, your energy, and your essence for its own benefit *(see You're Programmed on page 12)*. You may not have ended up where you thought you would because, under those influences, you were working toward something that was not aligned with you or, like the American Dream, was largely based in fantasy to keep you chasing something outside of you.

When you begin to realize that you may have been tricked somewhere along the way, you're likely going to feel betrayal, anger, or frustration. Maybe you've been working a corporate job for some time, climbed the corporate ladder to look around and think, *This is it!?* Or you've been working so hard to get that ONE moment – up on stage, winning that award, getting married – and suddenly you're there, then the moment passes, and you think, *Now what?* Maybe things have always flowed for you and you just want to keep that expansion rolling. Great, there's space for everyone here.

Wherever you find yourself on that spectrum, you're here now, holding this book, reading these words that will hopefully help launch you into the next leg of the journey. You might master everything in this book (a boy can dream), but still the journey goes on. That's how it works here; life never stops life-ing. To navigate with grace and create intentionally, we need to center ourselves, focus our energy, and build from there.

If you feel a little lost or lonely, embrace it. If you feel ready to move on from something, or someone, accept it. That's the first step toward creation. If you feel empowered, excited, or aligned – amazing. Own it. Wherever you are right now, own it.

Acceptance of where we are allows us to take ownership over our creative power and that ownership allows us to pivot. We can't go anywhere if we avoid looking at where we are currently. Acceptance alone will begin to open any blocked energy, it'll invite in awareness of what needs to change and allow you to channel through new ideas, energies, and intentions. Avoidance won't.

Read that again.

Maybe we feel amazing. Maybe we built something beautifully aligned, and it's meant to be ours. Awesome. I'm sure we all have a few of these things in our lives. Maybe we feel like we've put in a lot of effort, but nothing really changed, we're not any happier, and we're wondering why the fuck we put so much into something. We might obsess about the waste of time, energy, money, everything. But regardless of the outcome, it's the result of our energetic contribution. If what's in front of you feels expansive and brings peace, flow, and joy, you're likely building toward something that was truly meant for you. If it feels bumpy, rough, and draining, you might be barking up the wrong tree. Some friction is okay – it helps nudge us in the right direction, it shapes new ideas, and we find solutions that lead us toward aligned success. But friction every day, all day, that's keeping you in a state of constant turbulence, stress, and frustration is not the vibe, babe. Something is off. You either need to pivot how you're doing it, or pivot what you're doing and try something new entirely.

It's important to review what we're getting back from all we're giving. We invest our time, focus, energy, actions, money, love, and momentum into people and processes, and then we get a result, whether we're pleased with that result or not. The mechanism works. Investments = results (both good and bad). That's the takeaway. You are able to use that same mechanism, that focus, that energy, that momentum, to build the life you want, from an aligned place, and to find equally aligned results that feel great, but only you can ask, 'Is the juice worth the squeeze?'

The fact that you created your own mess might be a bit of a hard pill to swallow. Or maybe it's intimidating knowing that you have to take responsibility for who you are, what you want, and what you need to do to get wherever you want to be, but that's also empowering. At the end of the day, everything that got you to this point was a contribution. How *you* responded to things. The path *you* chose, the life *you* built. If you acknowledge your responsibility, and your ability to build something regardless of how you feel about it, that acknowledgement is the key to your power. You had a choice in the past and you have a choice now. And that means you can choose something else.

this is the groundwork to creating your reality.

Before the mind discounts this conversation by over-identifying with struggles, or past traumas, or layers of socio-economic issues, intersectionalities of barriers, race, gender, disabilities, etc., I think it's important that we all recognize that consciously or unconsciously, knowingly or unknowingly, we invested, to some degree, in the ideas or systems that were placed upon us. We have been trained. We have been conditioned. We have been programmed a certain way to just accept these things as they are and even just admitting that takes audacity, so we start there. That takes courage. By doing that, we're already starting to live differently. We see ourselves as a co-creator – now we can co-create something else. By understanding this, we can experiment with doing things differently.

You already know how to co-create your reality. You've done it. That's how you got here. You might look around and feel trapped, but what if all these years have been training for you to learn how to escape? The systems that are taking advantage of you have unknowingly taught you everything you need to turn that poison into medicine and create the life you want.

When you step out of the 'woe is me' bullshit (and sometimes it takes years to let it go, I've been there), you're gonna build your new reality using all the same skills you've already perfected. You didn't lose anything, you're changing direction. Don't get me wrong, shit happens and we are all victims at times, to varying degrees, and I don't think we can or should bypass that. But ask yourself how much longer you're willing to invest in that story.

You're Programmed

(well, the Self is...)

So am I.

We all are, and the sooner we stop thinking this is a conspiracy theory, and we accept that we are impressionable beings, the sooner we can do something about it. We can reshape our mind and anchor into our own, liberated programming.

Somebody somewhere created systems to serve themselves. Not everyone, not everywhere, and not *every* system, but a lot of the big ones. For starters the capitalist economic systems, institutionalized religions, industrial education models, law and policing systems, housing and land ownership models, privatized and gatekept healthcare structures, mainstream media conglomerates, surveillance technology, social media algorithms, and all major global trade and resource extraction networks... but who's counting? Some of these systems – just play with the idea with me for a minute – figured out a way to harvest our energy for their benefit. Picture this. Someone plants seeds in your garden. You grow the seeds. You nurture them, water them, and grow them. You weed the shit outta that garden, and 'they' show up and take the fruit.

I promise it gets lighter

Now I know tHiS sOuNdS WiLd but let's zoom in on one example to simplify things. We isolate ourselves in bed scrolling on a phone chasing a dopamine hit over and over and over again. Or we binge six hours on Netflix until the 'Are You Still Watching?' prompt pops up because even the TV is thinking, *Fuck babe, you're still here?* Yes, I'm still watching. No, I didn't leave the house with the TV on. I'm literally rotting on my couch and you're interrupting *Love Is Blind,* Season 8, Episode 110, you jerk.' So, we reach for the remote and we press play.

Let's say you spent 15 hours this week glued to the screen one way or another. (That's probably a gross underestimate. Check your screen time and report back. Seriously. Write the number ____) That's your energy. Gone. That's your precious time. GONE. And y'ain't gettin' it back, babe. She's gone with the wind. But you know who made money from that? Netflix. Instagram. Meta. The manipulative motherfuckers we keep crawling back to like a toxic ex. They're literally selling that data, likely tracing your behavior, and making money from advertisers. They're cashing in on *your* most vital resources – your time and energy. If that's not considered 'harvesting' your energy, then I don't know what is. And honestly, I don't care what you wanna call it, it's happening. The truth is the truth. When we sit there pulled into the vortex of hypnotic television, social media, and movies, we're a crop being harvested. I know this and I still go back. I just create boundaries so my screentime isn't 14 hours a day (anymore).

No Shame!

I watched a documentary about the structure of modern elementary schools and how they were designed around the 19th-century factory system. Lining up in silence, fixed schedules, bells, breaks, uniforms, desks, and even the mundane memorization of content was created to condition students into obedience, punctuality, and comfort with supervision, preparing them for factory work and desensitizing them to boring environments void of creativity and color. The goal was to create compliant workers by the masses. Who the fuck is that benefitting? Not me. I hated school – so did most of us. This is why Ms. Cox hated me so much. I spent 50 percent of my time from grades four through eight literally sitting in the hallway and learning by watching the class through the door. That breaks my little heart. That definitely didn't help my gay little psychic psyche's development of the 'I'm an outsider' program, but here we are.

Fuck some of those teachers – of course I was a rebel. I don't wanna work like that. I wanna be a tarot reader and apparently write a book one day. I wanna do mushrooms by the river and roll around with goats on Tuesday afternoons. I don't wanna eat a moist lunch out of a warm thermos and I don't care WTF you think about me. Come down to the river, trust me. The goats don't bite that hard.

I always knew I wasn't made to be clocking in. A white feather just fell from the sky and landed beside me as I type this. See, it's a sign. We're not meant to be factory workers indoors all day. We're meant for goats and feathers from the sky! *(Go to page 225 and read about Synchronicities.)*

Anyway, the people who created the structures you've trusted until now enlisted you to co-create *their* reality. These systems are not aligned with your natural state. They were not created to protect your wellbeing. These structures are not found in nature, not like this. They are manmade. And I don't mean that in a misogynist way like women couldn't have made them, I just think this type of extractive manipulative bullshit was *very likely* a man. There's no space for the divine feminine flow in a forceful structure like that. It's not aligned with our natural state (we all have both feminine and masculine energies by the way). That shit just ain't right. *Fuck that.*

Living in outdated, misinterpreted, and toxified structures and systems makes it hard to live a life aligned with your soul.

These systems are meant to confuse and control us. They're invisibly designed to keep us trapped. This is part of the reason why you can't trust everything that passes through your mind. Your mind has been conditioned by these outward forces – society, religion, culture, social media companies, x, y, z. All the messages we've gotten through music, Hollywood, and TV. It's not to say your mind is always wrong. Our minds are incredible, right? My mind allows me to connect with my spirit. It allows me to create. It allows me to appreciate art and music and dancing and nature and so much else around me, but sometimes it's terrible because the system is literally inside my mind. We need to actively decolonize our minds if we want to decolonize these structures *(see page 199)*.

The mind needs to be in service of the heart.

This is where our liberation lies.

Some of us need to grieve the time we lost while taking care of a garden we thought was ours but really wasn't. You tried hard. You watered the plants each day and pruned them as they grew. You followed all the rules. And now maybe you're realizing this isn't the harvest you wanted. This is part of the human experience. We grow and we change like the seasons. And we need to garden accordingly. So maybe it's time for change.

Time to uproot.

Time to replant yourself.

Maybe it's time to cry. *(See Grief and Releasing on page 110).*

And it's definitely time to rewild *(see page 133).*

↳ Important.

Microchips

I want you to imagine a sci-fi world. It's the year 3026 and we get microchipped in our brain right after birth. On our chip there's a program already installed and running – kinda like your iPhone software. Imagine a set of rules, guidelines, ideas, perspectives, language, limits, structures, and more. Like social norms. *Stay in line. Listen. Obey.* It's all you've ever known and it's all around you and it's everyone you know. Like a fish in water, you don't realize you're swimming inside these structures. Society, school, our family, friends, television, and culture – it all shapes a story in our head, a software that gets downloaded into our consciousness. And you live your life believing certain things about yourself and your reality. What's possible. What's not. What's allowed. What isn't. Your whole life externally reflects your inner understanding of what's available to you. And every day the people and experiences around you further confirm your reality by reinforcing it through groupthink, acceptable behaviors, celebrations, and a variety of controlled conversations.

If you're thinking this fantasy sounds a little too real and familiar, I would agree. There are definitely parallels to our own experience right now. That being said, let's imagine one day your microchip glitches and you get a taste of an alternative reality. Then let's pretend you get a glance at what's possible and you begin to intentionally seek answers and ideas outside of what's been 'allowed' or taught up until now. What if you begin to drift? Notice I didn't call it a 'U-Turn'? That's because a drift is much calmer. An intentional energetic drift.

iOS 2026

The intentional drift is an opportunity to side-slide into a new reality. Imagine the same routine every day: the same commute, the same conversations, the same microchipped program running on repeat. Now imagine creating a little bit of space between you and your automatic thoughts and actions – enough space to choose how you respond, rather than reacting as you always have. That's how you drift into a new reality.

It's kinda like taking the high road: not engaging in drama, or over-explaining yourself, not getting pulled into someone else's bullshit and cleaning it up. It's a gentle move toward calm, centered energy; a step closer to knowing your worth and choosing differently, not loudly, but energetically. Sometimes drifting means speaking up, owning your voice and saying something you once would have swallowed. But at its heart, a drift is a subtle energetic shift back into sovereignty. It's about aligning with who you want to be, not who you've been.

This is what people mean when they say there are infinite possibilities available at all times. It's also how I understand quantum leaps. Remember when you realized Santa or the Tooth Fairy wasn't real? Or when you clocked someone was lying to you? That's a paradigm shift. Something cracks open and you enter a whole new level of awareness.

So there it is, folks… I give you, *The Drifter*. And if you act now, you, too, can drift your way into a new reality!

How? By expanding your ideas, shifting your belief systems, and changing your actions. We also need to clear some space for that expansion. To do this, we need to explore our inner daemons, the energies that pulse through our reality and move through our body, and the dragons that run (or ruin) our life *(see page 85)*. If you control the dragons, you control the kingdom. Be Khaleesi, the Mother of Dragons.

"Default Settings" what are yours?

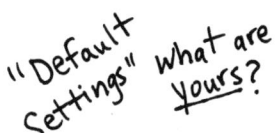

Lose Your Fucking Mind

You know sometimes you hear people talk about someone and they're like, 'She lost her mind'? It's always said as something negative. Well, I say – lose it, babe! Let it all go. Sometimes we need to look at things with that Fuck It energy *(see page 179)* and completely fall apart.

They lost their damn mind!

No, they lost the *mind control* that convinced us adults shouldn't have fun. They lost their mind and found their fuckin' soul! Maybe we'll find them dancing down the aisles of a grocery store. Smiling. Enjoying the mundane tasks and fully living life again! That's an inner child activation and that's the first way back to a truly liberated experience: play. Remember when you used to *really* play? Have you tried recently not caring about what people think?

Imagine, you see a woman really shakin' her thang walking past the frozen fish section at your local grocers. She heard a song that reminded her of high school back when she was awkward with braces and too-long limbs and no one ever asked her to dance. And you know what? Now, no one needs to! She doesn't need to be asked. She doesn't need permission, or invitation. Maybe she's still awkward, who fucking cares!? She's gonna dance the hell out of 'Mr. Brightside' down the cereal aisle and she's gonna forget to grab milk! She'll get home to some dry-ass cereal but at least she had a good time.

Then we've got Carol, over in the cheese department, who's having a full-blown identity crisis because the gouda sold out and she planned her entire evening around that recipe. Now she's cross-referencing ingredients and piecing shit together like she's trying to crack the Da Vinci Code because she's so stuck in the same damn loop that she can't imagine changing gears, switching directions, or trying something new. Dinner is ruined, Carol. You failed us all. No, seriously, babe, you need to chill the fuck out. Grab a different cheese. Move on. But she can't. She couldn't possibly change the recipe. Her fragile grip on 'what should be' might shatter if things don't go as planned. And then what? The rest of her reality starts to unravel and she has to process the emotions she's been dodging since 1996. Dear God, Carol, FIND THE FUCKING GOUDA! See how quickly our micro-management of what should be can snowball into full blown lactose lunacy?

So, who are *you*? Are you Carol, or are you the one who apparently lost their mind? I'd rather be the one dancing down the frozen fish aisle if I'm being honest. Carol sounds like a nightmare and, gouda or not, I think she needs a therapist before she needs another dinner guest.

Anyway, who here *really* lost their mind?

Don't be Carol.

Judgment

Judgment is a sneaky snake. Judgment fills the gap between what you think you know but actually don't, and it leaves no space for curiosity or connection. Whether it's a person, a place, or a thing, judgment creates an assumption that you know something you don't. Judgment sneaks in and steals our chance to know something we thought we already knew. So now we *think we know* what we don't know, which tricks us into not knowing what we *should* know. Basically, judgment hijacks knowledge: We think we know something, when *really* we know nothing, and now we don't know what we don't know. It's kinda wild, you know?

I'm noticing recently that I cast judgment on so many random things. Objects, people, ideas, music, television, cars — it's an automatic filing system that my brain has learned as an adaptive tool to keep me safe. Judgment is at odds with curiosity, which is the root of play, creativity, and connection, and it robs us of all three.

We inherit many of the beliefs that guide our judgments from society and family; they are even shaped in part by our genetics and epigenetics *(see Decolonization of the Mind on page 199).* In early childhood we're like sponges, soaking things up with no filter or way to understand what's true or false. Our consciousness is shaped by what our caregivers consider to be 'good' or 'bad.' We begin to understand which behaviors will be rewarded and which ones punished as we receive praise for some things and warnings or scoldings for others.

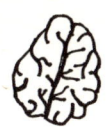

Over time our brains wire themselves for efficiency, not fairness. Quick judgments help us preserve energy for survival. Remember we're still working with the same hunter/gatherer brain that we had thousands of years ago. These shortcuts help us identify friend or foe.

In tribal times being cast out was terrifying. What would you do for food? Safety? No protection or food = death. We're still working with that brain. There's even a lingering fear of being associated with certain people, things, or ideas because we don't want to be mocked, rejected, or cancelled – effectively 'thrown out of the tribe.' All those outcomes are linked to a lack of safety. Feeling unsafe triggers fear. The idea of something new or unplanned can also trigger fear in a lot of us. The amygdala is the threat detection center in the brain and it makes split-second decisions to keep us alive – but we can't always trust those decisions. Our fears distort our thinking. Sometimes the stranger on the street is just being nice and not sizing you up to rob you blind. Sometimes our judgments are wrong.

And sometimes judgments are bang on – this is when intuition and awareness are fully aligned. We *can* judge things, in fact, we *should* judge things. Driving your car off a cliff is not helpful if you want to live a long, healthy life. That's a *good* judgment call; welcome to discernment. Picking up dog shit at the park and throwing it at the lady with the yappy little Pomeranian is a *bad* judgment call. My point is judgment is a good thing when used properly; avoiding a sketchy alley at night, assessing the weird energy of someone who's trying to manipulate you, recognizing when certain people are draining your energy or taking advantage of you. We want to hold onto that ability for discernment. But judging things simply based on a hardwired survival mechanism won't necessarily serve you. So, we have to learn how to tell the difference.

If you, like me, experienced some weird ass shit as a child then you may also be hardwired for survival. That's a trauma-response, babe. You might be quick to ask yourself: *Am I safe here? Is this person a predator, enemy, or foe?* I love my protective brain, but that guy drives me absolutely insane sometimes. For a long time it was like every person, environment, or situation I found myself in had this underlying energy of, *How do I avoid danger?* We don't need to be focused on this death-by-tiger energy like some of our ancestors were. Instead, we might be more concerned with a social death, which can feel just as scary in the mind and body. Again, being cast out. Your mind might work like this to some degree:

Keyword: "perceived"

Quick Judgments = Control = Perceived Safety

And maybe that, over time, became your baseline. We can begin to override our automatic operating system with a more soulful experience. Healing requires rewiring, which can happen through awareness and repetition of new behavior. I'll expand more on this in some of the QR code resources.

It's possible to consciously rewire and liberate yourself from these programs; I'm still working on it, but I've come a really long way. In doing so, I have found a lot more space for curiosity, connection, creativity, and playfulness. And you can, too.

Here's some support. ➔

People Are Trees

If you can, look at a tree. It can be any tree. A cedar. A palm tree. A Baobab tree like in *The Little Prince*. Seriously, get up and find one, bring this book.

Now put the book down, take five full breaths while looking at the tree, then come back and continue reading.

Did you notice yourself when observing the tree? Were you judging it for not being big enough or projecting onto it what it should look like? Did you make fun of the tree and belittle it or shame it, or were you just observing it and letting it be exactly what it is? Did you wish the tree was a flower? Or did you let the tree be the tree that it is?

This is how we need to look at people.

They are who they are. Let them be who they are, and place them in your life accordingly. Stop judging them for being human *(see Judgment on page 20)*. Stop trying to make them something they're not. Observe and allow. Don't try to control them, change them, or fix something you think needs fixing. Instead, control yourself and control where you place yourself, and control the types of relationships you let influence your life. *(See Change Your Environment, Not Yourself on page 138)*. Change your location, or boundaries, or mindset.

This is about taking ownership over your own feelings. It's about your agency. It's almost *never about them*. When we make it about them, we give our power away. We let their actions, or inactions, dictate our wellbeing. Stop letting external things control your emotional state. The passive aggressive co-worker who insulted your shirt? The lady at the grocery store causing a scene? None of these things should shake you because they're not about you. So don't waste your energy trying to make sense of nonsense or trying to control other people or an outcome. Stop judging it as good or bad, right or wrong. Just let it be and move on. Protect your energy and save it for yourself.

If your emotional state is based on everything around you being perfect then you're going to live a hard life. If staying home alone is the only way to maintain peace, then you're missing the point of these practices. This book is not intended to have you isolating yourself so nothing can touch you. That's avoidance and mental fragility. This book and the practices beyond these pages are meant to help you navigate your life in a more grounded way, so you understand yourself and can recalibrate your mental, emotional, energetic, spiritual, and physical health in a way that helps you manage life while staying anchored into the energy of your choice.

 That's liberation. That's freedom and that's intentional creation. And you can't get there if you're judging, projecting, or blaming every person for their behavior or trying to shape people into something they're not. Sometimes a bonsai just needs to be a bonsai. People are trees, ok? That's a Golden Rule. Let them be trees.

If you're feeling kinda corky, maybe branch out and meet Gloria (*see page 134*).

 # Bending Time

Think about something you need to do that makes you feel stressed or anxious. This is your mind travelling into the future and experiencing one future possibility in the now. Think about a major regret, a painful experience, or an opportunity missed. This is your mind travelling back into the past. But none of this energy is as 'fixed' as we tend to believe it is. We can shift our perspective on what happened and release the intensity of the future or past experience by sitting with it, moving it, and reshaping our relationship to it.

This is rewriting the story.

When your mind goes back to the past or forward to the future, you're experiencing that moment in the body, right? That's why you feel the knot in your stomach. The body stores energy and memory. You can also work with your body to help release stuck energy from your past or shake things up to shift your future. This is how we heal ourselves in multiple timelines: future, past, and present. This is how we create more intentionally. It's all far more malleable than we've been led to believe.

Modern science shows through quantum physics that particles exist in multiple states until they are observed. Research like the delayed-choice experiment and the quantum eraser experiment show us that how we observe a particle now can determine what it did in the past. This suggests time may not be strictly linear. This means shifting our perspective on what has been can reshape our experience of the past and the outcomes of it in the now. In physics, retrocausality – the concept that the future can influence the past – shows that time isn't strictly moving in one direction. Neuroscience has proven that reframing memories literally rewires your brain and nervous system, creating new emotional responses and patterns, which ripple out into the present moment, and therefore could potentially alter future decisions and behaviors.

I want to go a layer deeper here and get into some really woo-woo shit, so just come along for the ride.

This is Amazing

Retrocausality suggests that there's a future timeline; you in the future somewhere, living your best life, for example, and that future version of you is sending signals back to this present-day version of you. So, imagine you're somewhere in the future living your dream life – healthy, rich, sexy AF, taking time to rest, cooking dinner with fresh herbs from your garden, you know? The good life. And the version of you right now, reading this book, is receiving the hints that would help you get there. The future you is sending gut feelings, ideas, and clues as to how you can start living that life. Imagine the version of you now merging with the future version through a cute lil' scavenger hunt called life.

Have you ever felt that pull to do something you can't really explain? That's you, the future you, pulling you toward becoming you, in the future. Technically, that future version of you led you to this book so you could grasp a deeper understanding on how to connect to that future you, so the present you can pull that future timeline into the present moment and collapse the separation between you now and future you. There's a version of you who has already read this, and you're merely catching up. There's a version of me who has already finished writing this book. Who's already done and thinking, *Wow, what a great book.* I can energetically feel what the future version of this book feels like.

I'm downloading the words from my future self and typing them in the present.

Your future self knows it's real, and that's why they pulled you into reading this book. To shift your reality.

It works both ways. Future to the present. Present to the future. Time is not linear and it's not real – not in the way you think it is. It's not just a manmade clock on the wall in constant progression. You *are* moving through sequences of experiences and different layers of the now. We're updating our present reality through presence, and decisions, and how we relate to the future. But time is spiralic and seasonal, not linear. It loops and folds in on itself in various ways. We don't move forward, we move inward and outward, and we return to familiar frequencies with a new layer of awareness. This is why we can go back into memories and re-relate to those experiences, rewriting the narrative and reshaping our now from that restructuring of the past. Likewise, we can visit the  future and adjust our experience of it by cultivating the energy now, in preparation for the experience.

Maybe something feels overwhelming. You can use your body to move and shake that energy until it feels less intense *(see page 42)*. You can use your brain to visualize your desired outcome *(see Intention Setting on page 232)* and then activate your emotions to help anchor the body into that energetic state *(see page 171)*. This is how we create intentionally.

Pro athletes and high-impact individuals use visualization (a mode of meditation) to prepare themselves for games, speeches, and more. They tap into the future experience they desire and visualize it clearly. They then bring the feelings and emotions from the future into the present, so they can feel it fully in the body. They experience winning, nailing that speech, getting the promotion, or whatever it is. They use their body in the present moment to experience the energy of what it is they want to happen in the future by intentionally attuning their energy, tuning their emotions (energy in motion = e-motion) into their desired outcome. They act and feel as if it's happening right now.

Feel it until it's real; that's the deal.

This practice supports the co-creation process (bringing forth the reality we want) and it also helps to alleviate fears, stress, and other interferences.

Now let's play.

STFU for one whole day! → **observe your thoughts**

Spend time alone!

Movie — solo trip — dinner

Dance in Public. ♪♫

create one new daily ritual. ♥

→ Sit in a cafe and observe people; make **zero** judgements. **Simply observe.** ☺

TRY SOMETHING NEW

Delay your **first** reaction.

Set a timer for 15 min. Don't stop **writing!**

What stories keep coming up? Notice them & keep track of the **themes.**

* Speak **less**, Listen **more**. shhh!

? Question one strong belief. ?

Take a new way to work.

Don't listen to their Advice.

* Ask yourself **"why"** you **think that.**

WOW!

(PART TWO) THE AUDACITY TO FEEL IT ALL!

This part of the book is an invitation to actually feel your shit. I'm not just talking about grief or heartbreak. This is permission to experience real joy without guilt. Pride without ego. Pleasure without a sense of shame or a deep fear of losing it all. The deeper we allow ourselves to feel, the stronger we become. When we lean into our emotions, we create more space for real intimacy and deeper connections. We find more expansive opportunities and true alignment with our own unique nature. It invites a renewed sense of creativity and play. We find flow. True flow. We simply cannot reach our fullest potential by avoiding any parts of ourselves. Finding true success comes from allowing all parts of you to be seen, heard, and felt. And that starts with you.

There's a wild kind of courage in letting yourself go there – in feeling everything so deeply in a world that would rather keep you quiet, clean, and in-line. Most of us are scared to speak up. Most of us spend our entire lives running from ourselves, and I hate to be the bearer of bad news, but y'aint going anywhere, babe.

Wherever you find yourself, you'll find yourself there. So you might as well enjoy it (or cry it out or whatever). For so long, I carried this unsettling feeling that I tried to outrun. Maybe you feel it in your nervous system sometimes, too? Like a deep sense that something is wrong, a feeling of anxiety, or other sensations that seem to come from nowhere. Those are trapped emotions, and we can un-trap them. They can't be outrun, so why not sit with them?

I promise, feeling the shit we've been avoiding for years will only release the pressure. It'll create more space for all the good emotions to return or expand. And we all have it; we're human. We're here to feel it all. So let's find more laughter, more smiles, more tears, and more screams. Let's feel it all so we can be truly and utterly alive. That's a life worth living.

You're stronger than you think – and if I made it this far, babe, you'll be just fine!

So, settle in. Let that shit move through you. The good, the bad, the ugly. It won't kill you, I promise. In fact, it'll make you feel more alive.

Your Body Is Technology

Your body is the highest form of technology on the planet. It heals itself. It helps you co-create your reality. It repairs and builds, purges and cleans. Like an antenna, it helps you interpret the energy in your environment, it can enhance and adjust your energetic state – and so much more.

It's incredible, and it's always communicating with you. You just need to learn how to listen. It's kinda like astrology – once you understand the language, you're working on a whole other level of reality.

Your Body Needs Support ✱

First and foremost, the body needs care and support. We need to eat, sleep, shit, shower – you know the drill. Before we can lean into all the gifts of the body, the ones that come online when we're regulated and in a state of safety, trust, and flow, we need to make sure our Hierarchy of Needs is met. It's hard to step out there with your high kicks and jazz hands if you're in a constant state of survival, so let's get the foundation right first.

A man named Abraham Maslow created a psychological theory of motivation often used by teachers in the classroom. According to Maslow's Hierarchy, our basic needs of survival – physiological needs like water – need to be met before we can fulfill the needs that fall into more abstract categories. Maslow's pyramid of needs puts physiological needs on the bottom (food, water, shelter). This forms the base of the pyramid and is the foundation upon which everything else is built. Next comes 'Safety and Security,' which includes things such as family and health. In the middle you have 'Love and Belonging', a sense of community, intimacy, and connection. Second to the top is 'Self-Esteem,' which encompasses confidence, self-trust, and respect. Finally at the top is what he calls 'Actualization', which is where you get to a larger meaning and sense of purpose. So, before we can fully work with the power of the body, or find incredible flow, or activate an insane level of abundance into our lives, we need to ensure we have the foundation to grow. So, have you even had enough water today? Do you have a community, or at least a few good friends? Once we've got the basics down, we can activate a whole other level of expansion, creation, connection, and play.

Your Body Communicates

Discomfort is data.

The body feeds us information. Do you feel uncomfortable? Great – that's data. What's active and alive in you? What energy needs to move out and through?

Are you feeling creative and expansive? Perfect. Lean into it. Do you feel contraction in some way, in some environments, or around some people? That's likely rejection or redirection. Honor it. Constriction? That sense of wanting to retreat alone? That's your body trying to protect you. Or leading you to rest.

Before our mind can logically uncover the truth, our body has often figured it out. Our body is reading the energy and interpreting it to us through sensations. Our body is experiencing an invisible layer of reality that doesn't always make sense to us mentally. The issue is that most of us want to fuck around and find out. Have you ever dated someone you felt like you shouldn't only to say, 'I fucking knew it!' weeks later? Exactly. You already knew it in your body. You could feel it, but mentally they checked all the boxes. You can avoid this. You can use your body like a pendulum to understand what, for you, is a 'yes' or a 'no.' What feels right and what feels wrong. *(See more on this in The Body Can Guide You section.)*

Your Body Is an Alchemist

Movement is medicine.

Your physical body is a tool for alchemy. You can use it to shift your energetic state. If you're scared, stressed, or overwhelmed, MOVE: jump, dance, scream, cry, paint, laugh, sing, sail – do whatever you need to do to move the energy *(see Alchemize Energy, page 49)*. Just move it.

After a few minutes of moving your body or taking some kinda of action, you'll likely notice yourself dropping out of the mind and into the body. The intensity will begin to shift and the energy becomes less dense.

Don't you feel better after you scream 'FUCK!' ten times at the top of your lungs in your car? Maybe that's just me. I bet you feel a bit better after you cry though, right? That's your body releasing what was stuck. Ever punched a pillow and then felt a strange sense of relief right after? That's a recalibration from anger or frustration back into peace, or at least a step toward it. This is how we regulate our nervous system. The energy arrives, and we move it. Whatever caused the stress can suddenly seem lighter, or like it has less power over you. Because it does. Because you took back your power by working with the emotions and you shifted your state of being. Good job.

Your Body Can Guide You ↰ *but are you listening?*

Your body already knows the answer.

At the heart of this book are the questions: *How can I enjoy my life a little more? How can I manage my own shit? How can I move through life with ease and flow?* One answer: Pay attention to your body.

Think of someone you love, or a beautiful dream or goal you have for yourself. Seriously, take a minute and experiment with this. Put down the book, sit back, and feel into your dream, then come back. Notice the shift? Maybe things felt softer. Lighter. More expansive. Now think of something that hurt you in the past. A betrayal, a major loss. Notice how your body responds – a small contraction, a ping, a sense of 'ick.' *try it!*

This is a great way to begin to understand what you're feeling. What does expansion feel like? What does contraction feel like? Which feels like a 'yes'? Which feels like a 'no'? Play with it. This can guide you forward.

This is how we begin to work with the body as a guide. These expansions and contractions are signals that lead us toward what's aligned. With practice, you'll get a clearer answer. You can always slow down, breathe, and feel into questions like:

- Do I really need to eat this?

- Should I accept this opportunity?

- Is this person aligned with me?

The more you practice, the stronger the communication gets. This is how we learn the language of our body, understand the desires of the soul, and guide our self and soul back into alignment.

Your Body Can Be Reprogrammed

Think about what trained and conditioned your body. What habits and rhythms were maybe picked up in your younger years that are still stickin' around? What behaviors do you keep going back to? What do you reach for, even if it doesn't serve you? Think of your body as a beautiful machine — the original software was downloaded by an external source, shaped by your environment, and programmed by your genetic, epigenetic, and generational coding *(see You're Programmed, page 12)*. The software was updated, at different points in time, with coping mechanisms, habits, and ways of moving through life. At some point we need to take inventory of what we do and why. I smoked a shit-ton of weed in college and my body got used to it. It was an automatic daily routine. I was on autopilot until I realized one day that a 33-year-old pothead slurring my words at Burger King isn't as cute as it once was. We need to clear out and update our programming every so often. We interrupt our internal knowledge system and innate ability to flow through life when our outdated habits, programs, and rhythms are self-destructive, or simply not serving us any longer. We need to stop using the body for pleasure, escapism, or creating something from a conditioned place. Instead, let's begin to free the body, to liberate our behavior, and to move with a deeper connection to the soul.

We can train the body to be in support of the life we want to build and this type of coherence between the mind, body, and soul is extremely important in building the life we desire. So how do we do that? We interrupt the pattern. We pivot. We'll talk about this more on page 64 but for now, just know it's possible and maybe begin to ask yourself, *'Where is my body still moving through outdated programs and rhythms?'*

We want to learn to observe the mind and the body, and reprogram them.

What do you really want to reach for?

What do you really want to do?

The answers are inside you. Cliché, but true!

Nervous System 101

There was a time when I realized that I always felt anxious or like I was chasing something outside of me. Like I was plugged into an electric socket and couldn't figure out how to calm the fuck down. I had this sense of urgency or running out of time. Naturally this led to self-soothing, which led to overconsumption, overindulgence, and overextending myself (not a cute look). Over time, I became reliant on these things as a means of relief, and that eventually calcified into my behavior, my energy field, and my emotional response patterning as addiction. Addiction to drinking, drugs, sex, shopping, coffee, food... anything to make me feel better. Anything to stop the electric pulse that I could not actually identify. Anything for a minute of rest and relaxation – and even then, was I *really* relaxing or was it just momentary relief.

The truth is my nervous system was totally shot from years of bullshit, childhood trauma, family drama, bullying, and escapism. Does *everyone* feel like this? Honestly, in this day and age, yeah, a lot of people feel like this, but does that make it right? Nope. So how did we get here? Constant stress leads to burnout and issues with our mental and physical health. When we're stuck in survival mode, from anything like childhood trauma or growing up poor, we aren't able to create a stable enough environment, or calm enough nervous system, to comfortably grow. We overreact to the small stuff and get caught in drama triangles. *(Take a look at the Drama Triangle on page 114.)* We can't create our authentic reality when we're not rooted in physical and emotional safety.

So how do we help ourselves?

A regulated nervous system is the foundation of co-creating your desired reality. You can't really do that if your nervous system is a rampant beast running the show with chaos. If you're feeling unsafe then you will likely make decisions from a wounded space. How can you create a sense of security and expansion from a place of contraction and instability? It's not an energetic match. First, we need to learn how to cultivate a deep sense of trust in ourselves. We need to curate an environment that provides us with a sense of safety. We need stability so we can root down, then bloom up and out. When we are centered, we can anchor down into a desired state and we can create something greater *(check out Anchoring Your Energy on page 171)*. To center ourselves, we need to slow down. We need to find a sense of peace.

It's important to note: Regulating our nervous system doesn't always feel good, in fact, sometimes we need to feel bad, or sad, or angry. Regulation comes from moving the energy and feeling the emotions, not avoiding them. I feel great after I lose my shit in the car, or ugly cry on the shower floor. Fuck, put me on a trampoline and give me six minutes with a 160BPM track and I'll bounce this ass, flail these limbs, and fart my way to feelin' like a brand-new man. That'll regulate yuh real good! But don't worry, not all my methods are gassy.

My Go-To Nervous System Regulation Tools

- **Breathe** – Take slow, deep breaths while focusing on your root chakra (red in color at the base of your spine). You can also try box breathing (4 seconds in, hold for 4 seconds, 4 seconds out, hold for 4 seconds) and do that until you feel centered and calm.

(handwritten note: love this ↗)

- **Take a shake break** – Stand up and literally shake it out, shake it off, and shake it proud (or shake it sad, shake it anxious, shake it however you need to, just shake what your mama gave ya). Likewise, put on your favorite song and shake that ass. Shake something! For at least 5 minutes. Then, afterwards, settle into your breath (see above).

- **Try the classic 5-4-3-2-1 grounding technique** – Take yourself through your 5 senses one by one, naming 5 things you can see, 4 you can hear, 3 you can feel, 2 you smell and 1 you taste. (That last one can be hard sometimes. Unless you're a perpetual gum-chewer!) The goal is to bring your attention back to your senses, not your thoughts.

- **Scream your fucking ass off** – I normally do this in my car, into a pillow, or underwater.

- **Sleep better** – For real. Go to bed early and get seven–nine hours of sleep regularly. No screens an hour before bedtime! Instead, try journaling, coloring, puzzles, or something similar.

- **Kick the shit outta something** – Like, not a person, though. I love kickboxing, padel, and I've been known to beat up a punk-ass pillow rather well.

- **Eat real, grounding foods** – If it came out of a package, don't eat it. Avoid coffee and skip the booze. Think warm soup, mushrooms, oats, potatoes, or whatever else grows in the earth. It'll literally ground you. Stay away from spice and smoke (it activates fire and air).

one day a week to no tech!

- **Take a serious break from scrolling, from screens, and from input** – No podcasts. No music. Just nature – sit outside with the birds. Chirp chirp, babe.

- **Cry** – put on a sad playlist, sad movie, or just sit in your own little sob story and just cry your fucking eyes out. I have a stellium in Cancer. I LOVE a dramatic cry. ♋

The goal is to get out of the mind, back in your body, and feel what needs to be felt. It'll pass, I promise, and you'll feel SO much better afterwards. We want to be regulated as best we can, as often as we can. From there, we can create a real sense of safety, and from that safe place we can intentionally co-create our desired reality using the other practices in this book. Exercise and movement burns off stressful energy. Screaming helps clear the static. A quiet and clean environment helps balance our mind. Healthy food stabilizes us, sleep resets our system, and breathing helps to anchor us into the present moment. This leads us to clearer decisions, less panic, more energy to focus on our goals and an overall healthier and happier, stronger vibe that attracts healthier people, better experiences, and opportunities to gently expand into our life. A regulated nervous system is the foundation of everything. If there's one thing you should look at, if there's one place you should start, it's here. Now take a second and breathe (or fart).

Let's Regulate

Pause with the Panic

What if instead of running away from panic, we paused, and we sat with it for a minute? Let's start with a small panic. Not like a break-up or losing a job. Something more like missing a train or losing a credit card; in either case, you'll survive.

When we enter a state of panic, it's more often than not rooted in a sense of fear or a complete lack of control. Something is happening that should not be happening, at least from our ego's perspective, and now we're entering uncharted territory. We're entering a whole new world. And not in good way like in *Aladdin*.

Whether big or small, a moment of panic is typically accompanied by the very real physical experience of activated survival mode — fight, flight, or freeze. We might sweat, we might cry. We might get those I'm-gonna-shit-myself-butterflies because our body is reacting to whatever we're experiencing as a very real threat, and the influx of energy needs an output. Yes, we need to move the energy. That doesn't mean skip over how you feel or bypass the experience, in fact pausing with the panic is the opposite of that. It means feeling it and doing something with it.

What if you don't think of panic as something you have to avoid but rather something you're meant to experience? What if we play with the panic?

Maybe, eventually, we even find pleasure in panic.

Stay with me on this, I know it sounds a lil' woo-woo. And it probably feels kinda weird to think of panic in pleasurable terms, but we're not afraid of weird, are we? Maybe you are afraid of weird, great – use that. Everything is data. Everything is material to work with.

Panic is rooted in the thought, *I don't know what's about to happen and I'm terrified of the potential outcome.* Well, if something is out of your control, how liberating. Of course there are real moments of panic, like when you're making dinner and your sizzling fajitas sizzle a lil' too high and light your kitchen on fire – it's real, it's time-sensitive and it's situational. That'll get your cortisol and adrenaline spiking real quick, and for good reason. But then there's perceived panic. It's like an imagined emergency, a fantasy, or emotional threat. Like sending that risky text and not getting a reply. Your mind can't always tell the difference between a real threat and an emotional threat so your body may respond the same. Tight chest, sweaty palms. The difference is that you're not reacting to what's actually happening, you're reacting to what this reminds you of. A deeper unprocessed part of yourself. This is where you set yourself free and connect deeper with trust. Trust is the cure for panic. You're freaking out over data – but data is mostly neutral until you give it a name and feeling. Like a computer, your subconscious is opening an old file folder and pulling out emotional data, only you don't know the script it's following. 'This makes me feel like the time I wasn't safe when X happened.'

Have you ever had one of those moments where your reaction doesn't quite match the experience? Like an overdramatization of something that in hindsight was pretty small? It's like all that energy, the emotional charge from the first time it happened, long ago and possibly out of your immediate memory, has returned. Boom. All at once you're freaking the fuck out or making something a big deal. It's fine, we've all been there. But when we panic our consciousness narrows, our body gets tight, and we enter a state of survival.

So, inhale.

And exhale.

Breathe back to your center.

Release all the feelings and stories and ideas of what could be.

Pause with the panic.

Remind your body that it's safe.

★ important

Even if things were to fall apart, or shit really does hit the fan, I want you to know you are now more experienced than ever before. You're better equipped, you have more resources, skills, and embodiment practices to ensure you pass through this easier, smoother, and bounce back quicker than the last time anything like this happened. So, own it. You've survived 100 percent of your bad days and you'll get through this one too.

You've got this.

And I'm right here with you on this one, babe.

Now sashay away.

Practice with the Panic

Your body is smart – it knows how to clear its own energy, kinda like when an antelope escapes death by lion, and then it does that cute lil' shake to recalibrate. Very Taylor Swift. We too need to shake when we get the shit scared outta us. We need to move that panic out of the body instead of pushing it down or avoiding it. We need to drop it like it's hot for the panic. We need to pussy pop with the panic. So, next time panic strikes, set a timer for five minutes and play in the panic. Freak the fuck out. Give yourself that five minutes to have your mini meltdown – scream, jump,

cry, run in circles around your unofficial emotional support dog, and then when the timer goes off, bring yourself back to a regulated state. Practice your box breathing or the 5-4-3-2-1 grounding technique (see page 42) to calm your nervous system.

Most of us are used to hearing 'Don't panic' or 'Calm down' when we find ourselves teetering on the edge, but what we actually need is permission to be where we're at. Don't calm down, panic. Then come back to center and pivot. Ownership of where we're at empowers us to change our state of being. Avoidance does not.

Panic can also sometimes feel good, safe, and familiar. I think lots of us are addicted to that panic cycle. The unconscious rush of endorphins and then the relief that follows when we do find our car or realize we didn't actually send the email, or still arrive on time (the best!).

We all know someone in our lives who's always running late. Late to the yoga class, late to the birthday party. Whatever it is. Maybe we get a flurry of frenzied text messages or maybe the late person doesn't bother to let us know. Either way they show up a little out of breath, radiant with a flush of panic. You cannot tell me they're not enjoying this! Even if there's embarrassment or guilt. After that comes relief. Maybe because no one is all that mad. Maybe because there's still time to order from the Happy Hour menu. Regardless, there can be an addiction to the rush, or to the panic, and if it remains unconscious, you'll keep manufacturing it yourself.

It's familiar. We *like* familiarity. It may be uncomfortable to be out of breath with everyone's eyes on you as you burst into the room, but there's a comfort to the discomfort. The addiction to that discomfort and the rush from chasing the clock, the panicked arrival, and the relief that 'I made it!' is quite literally a hormonal addiction in the body. Without awareness, the body will trick the mind into hijacking the experience to get that rush as often as needed. It's like when you know you're gonna be late but you keep watching the clock tick closer and closer, and you still haven't left yet. It's that build up. That's the body triggering stress chemistry in the brain to ensure the rush happens and all those endorphins get released. And just like that, you get your hit.

Give yourself space to start recognizing some of your patterns, habits, and reactions. We're aiming to observe them. Not to feel judged or ashamed. It's a moment to witness, and maybe to journal. This is how we create space for a shift.

So, what are your weird little addictions? (No shame)

— Alchemize Energy —

When the wheels fall off, life can be rough, babe. I get it. I used to drive a 2003 Ford Focus with a mirror that I duct taped to the side of my dented door. You know, the kinda car that pumps out hot air no matter how high you've cranked up the AC? Not cute. Some of these practices helped cool me down at that time (thank God). What a beautiful full-circle moment.

Here's a list of my top 10 ways to shift your energy when the Wi-Fi and your will to live both go out:

10 Ways to Shift Your Energy

1. **Move it** – I like to move it move it. Seriously dance, shake, jump.

2. **Breathe** – Put on a 5-minute timer and breathe. Your breath is always present.

3. **Write a letter to whatever the feeling is** – Ask why it's there, where it's from, or what it wants. Get it all out. Just start writing and keep going; don't stop and think.

4. **Pause with compassion** – The energy of compassion helps us accept whatever is happening. Just feel love for yourself and whatever's moving through you, regardless of what it is you're feeling.

5. **Laugh it off** – Take a moment to zoom out of the situation and just laugh at the comedy that's your life. How ridiculous it all can be.

6. **Phone a friend** – Sometimes we just need to hear the sound of someone we love, or to vent, bitch, or to just be witnessed. Beware of trauma dumping, not cute. Ask them if you can 'go off for a minute' and just let it rip if they have space and time.

7. **Hug a tree** – No, actually. Go out in nature and hug a fucking tree. Barefoot on the earth. Arms wrapped 'round. Cheek to bark. Breathe.

8. **BE STRESSED** – Sometimes you just need to be stressed. BE in it. Witness it. Ride it like a wave. Scream. Cry. Punch a fucking pillow.

9. **Connect with your senses and return to your body** – Light a candle or incense, take a cold shower, tap your body, have a tea, huff some essential oils, or step into the sun.

10. **Water and salt** – The ocean will help take it all away, just like our tears. I fucking love a good cry. And a salt bath, shower scrub, or foot soak. Gimme it all. I wanna cry in the salty tub. I have a cancer moon.

Shake That Ass

I hope you truly understand how magical your cute lil' body is. It can bypass the mind's need for control, and surrender into a space of expansion, nothingness, and silence. Movement has deeply shifted my reality. When we work with the body we open channels the mind can't. There are tons

true story

of somatic practices, but one of the easiest and most primal is dance. It doesn't need to be a two-and-a-half-minute choreographed jazz number to the *Lion King* that you force your sister to do in front of your parents in the basement with your black leather GORE-TEX boots on, but you do need to dance. Just move that body and you'll still get all the benefits. Even if your version of Simba will honestly never live up to mine.

Here's what's going on under the hood:

- **Full body memory activation** – Moving while we learn, like tapping and reciting affirmations for example, helps the mental input sink deeper into the memory by anchoring the concepts somatically.

- **Both hemispheres of the brain come online** – When we dance and move (especially with criss-cross type movements) we force the left and right brains to communicate, making it easier to connect new ideas later.

- **Nervous system reset and mental recharge** – Movement shifts us out of overdrive and into a more regulated state physically, while recharging our energy reserves and extending our attention span.

So, there it is. Another win for the mind-body connection, right? Experiment with it. Take a quick booty break. Go and choose a song, dance your ass off (high energy, non-stop, three minutes!), then come back.

Seriously. Take five minutes. Close this book and shake that ass.

Come shake that ass with me, babe!

Emotions: What Are They?

The emotion you feel moving through your body at any given time is literally energy in motion. E-Motion. Energy In Motion. I dabble with this idea when I talk about Dragons and Demons and how we can better work with our emotions *(see page 85)*. Emotions help us connect with our intuition, understand the shadow aspects in the subconscious that often run the show, and indicate what's truly in alignment with us and with what we want for ourselves.

We have primary emotions and secondary emotions.

Paul Ekman, a psychologist who believed that all human beings have biologically hardwired, universal, primary emotions, identified six: Happiness, Sadness, Fear, Anger, Disgust, and Surprise.

Michael Lewis later developed a list of secondary emotions that are shaped around the self-conscious experience of humans, including Guilt, Shame, Pride, Envy, and Embarrassment. He noted these are developed after our sense of self is established and are shaped by social norms.

Our primary emotions are like an instinct; they're universal and show up more immediately. Our secondary emotions are shaped by experience, culture, and context. They might arise with time. Happiness, a primary emotion, might signal safety and connection, while envy, a secondary emotion, is the culmination of fear, anger, and desire. Envy is rooted in the fear that we lack the ability to create something for ourselves that we see in others. This is likely rooted in a story you have about yourself (not being good enough, for example) that was shaped through a past experience, and you have defined yourself by it, claiming it to be true (when it is not in fact the ultimate truth, it is a perception). Regardless, the emotion is coming up. It is trying to reveal to you that something important is very much alive under the surface.

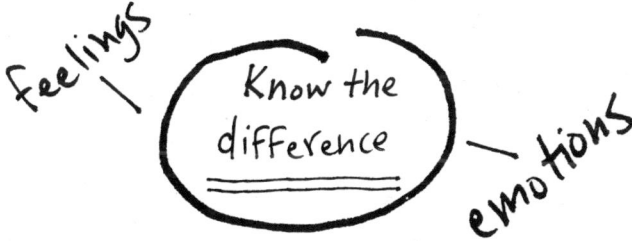

Emotions are data. They're showing us where we are in relation to people, experiences, and places. They are deeply rooted in the unconscious stories we believe about ourselves. Like our feelings, they are not always rooted in truth, although they are valid. It's important to understand that emotions are innate – they are a natural response to a situation or experience. Like an energetic impulse that moves through our energetic and emotional body and likely accompanies a physiological expression, like your heart racing, or sweat beading, when you experience fear. It's automatic and it's happening to you (or for you if you're looking through the lens of everything really serving your benefit).

Feelings are different, they are subjective labels we place on our experiences. Feelings are how we interpret the emotions running through us. Feelings are typically anchored into our reality after an experience has happened and we decide what we think it means, and how we think we are now, after it. It's kinda like the mechanism that helps us temporarily make sense of something, even if the story we're believing is not true, it's what we feel. Feelings shape our memories and our belief system, and our feelings and stories are hugely influenced by our culture, our religion, society, family, friends, and more. An emotion is short lived, but a feeling can last a lifetime.

The energetic movement of emotions stems from somewhere. The seed of that 'somewhere' was planted at some point in your life. That seed grew into a story that presents an idea of 'who you are' or 'what happened' or 'what that story means.' The reason I put these in 'quotes' is because it's not the reality. Yes, it may feel real, and your feelings are valid, but your feelings and the truth – the reality of the situation – are not always aligned. In short, you can't always trust your emotions, and you can't always trust the stories that your emotions tell. For example, someone gets busy and forgets to call you back. You have an emotional response – you get angry and annoyed. *They fucking forgot about me!*

The pain and frustration of that moment is rooted in a deeper story (maybe a few stories) from the past, that has you feeling that your needs aren't met or that others don't really care for you – *If they cared they would've called me back!* Let's say some kind of emergency happened, or they got busy at work, and that's why they didn't call. That has NOTHING to do with you. But your emotions are real, and that is what needs your attention. What energy is in motion, and why? What emotions are coming up? What is the story behind the emotions? Where has this happened before and why does it feel like it's happening again? This is where you are still trapped. These emotions are acting as a trigger helping you flag what is still stuck. Once you identify it, you can shift it and liberate yourself.

This is where the magic lies. Pain points are super helpful for you to clear out the old ideas, unprocessed shit, and limited perspectives that keep you trapped and out of alignment with your true self, your soul.

With emotions, we typically feel one thing because there's another thing that we're lacking. To simplify, our uncomfortable emotional states typically have an opposite emotion that can help us find balance again. For example, if you're feeling fear, you can lean into trust. If you're feeling lonely, you can seek connection. If you're feeling shame, you need acceptance. Grief, you need gratitude. Anxiety, you need presence and peace.

identify the root.

There can be a lot happening under the surface with any emotion, and often there's more than one thing moving. If you're feeling an energy of scarcity, then sit with it for a minute. Maybe you can't afford to join friends for dinner or you're unhappy with a cheap haircut or old, ill-fitting clothes you can't afford to replace (I've been there) – that feeling could be pointing you to look for more financial stability. It could activate feelings from childhood where there wasn't enough of something, where your needs were unmet, where you felt left out for whatever reason. This is the work – sitting with whatever is on the surface and exploring what's going on below it. You don't need to manage it all at once; you don't need to do a deep dive into all layers of this shit right away, just acknowledge it's there. Seeing it is half the battle. Do what you can to sit with it and feel it for a minute, let it move through you, then bring yourself back to center. Make a note of what you were feeling, and when you can, explore it deeper. Trust me, it'll be there, lurking in the shadows, until you sit with it and explore it deeper.

Remember, you are your own best friend, advocate, and caretaker. If something dense comes up, or you're in an emotional state, it helps to ask yourself what you really need in that moment. Can you identify the opposite feeling and try to work your way towards it? Often times, our pain is pointing us toward greater pleasure. The remedy, the medicine, is often hidden in the poison itself. It's like the echo of the cure. The wound is not a wall; it's a doorway that we can walk through if we can accept the

subtle hints and crack the code. Yes, babe, you're like a Rubik's Cube –
when it finally clicks, all the colors align and you feel whole again. So, ask
yourself, what's really going on backstage?

Let's say there's a secondary emotion presenting itself, a deep sense
of shame or embarrassment for something we've done. What's being
mirrored back to us in this experience? Maybe that embarrassment is
rooted in self-expression, because growing up your sibling, or someone,
made fun of you for your dancing, or singing, or painting, or however
you expressed yourself. A threaded, unconscious memory of when your
primary emotion, happiness, was thwarted by another person's judgment
or joke that made you shut down and feel inadequate. Welcome to the
shame party. Beneath the surface, you're questioning yourself, your
worth, and now have a feeling of inadequacy. Boom. Now you run into a
feeling of overwhelm. You need simplicity. If you're feeling judged, you need
acceptance. If you're resentful, you're asking for liberation and freedom of
expression. If you're feeling hopeless, you need purpose.

Tired? Rest.

Numb? You likely need more expression and less consumption.

This one specifically brings me back to the idea that when we're always
consuming, the consumption consumes us. It's fucking draining. We're
not meant to scroll, and read, and hear, and see more and more shit all
day. Opinions, fear, hooks, comments, likes, emails, texts, etc... it's too
fucking much.

If you're feeling numb, if you're drained by consumption, if
you're consuming all day, then go create something.

There are somatic practices that can also help you
ground deeper into the desired emotional state and there
are resources in this book to support that (see page 49).

Get off your phone.

Tell everyone to fuck off, and go paint, or sing, or dance.

Shift the energy.

Claim your peace.

Create something.

Let's dive deeper

WTF Am I Feeling and Why?

As we explored in Emotions: What Are They? on page 52, our emotions are a physiological response, an energetic pulse rushing through the body. Our feelings are the stories we attach to them. Emotions are experienced in the body. Feelings are experienced in the mind. Emotions are involuntary; we can't control them. Feelings are our interpretations of emotions. These interpretations are shaped by our wounds and by the beliefs we hold about ourselves, others, and the world around us. Feelings are stories, and our emotions activate them.

This is where it can get tricky. Sometimes we get so lost in our feelings that we can't find a way out. Our feelings, like our beautiful minds, can't always be trusted. I have four planets in Cancer, so my feelings absolutely love to tell a story (and not always a good one!). Sometimes we need to edit that script, babe. We can't always take the intricate rabbit holes we spiral down into at face value.

Feelings can help us create meaning around what we're experiencing, but they also reveal our subconscious fears, ideas, limits, and beliefs. For example, maybe someone triggers jealousy in you for a second. That jealousy might be rooted in a story that you'll never be as successful as they are. That story may point to a deeper belief that certain things aren't available to you, whether it be a car, a relationship, or a job. These limiting beliefs *can* be worked through. You can liberate yourself from them. I've done it.

How? By recognizing these loops, shifting your perspective, and rewriting the stories you've attached to your emotions. It's simple, but it's not always easy. This book is filled with practices and ideas that will help you do exactly that, though it will take some time.

This is exactly why working with your triggers is so powerful *(read Triggers and Flags (Pain Points) on page 71)*. Notice where you get caught up in stories about who someone is, what they did to you, or anything that feels like *this always happens to me!* We cycle through feelings that feel alive and real, even when the stories beneath them are shitty lies we've told ourselves. Emotions pass through us, but feelings can loop for years. Your nervous system will default to a familiar response until you re-pattern it. That doesn't make the stories true. Your feelings are valid, but the stories you tell yourself are entirely optional.

One of the simplest ways to interrupt these loops is to start paying attention to your stories. Honestly, tracking your stories, and the beliefs behind them, is a great way to identify where you're leaking energy, trapped in old thinking patterns, or still wounded in some capacity. Your stories may be rooted in faith, inspiration, and expansion, or in contraction, trauma, and survival patterns. When an emotion arises, ask yourself: *What's the root of this story?* Is it helping you create a life you want to live, or pulling you back into a victim state? Do you feel powerful or powerless?

Here's the key thing to remember: the emotional sensation may come back again in the future, but you can pivot your perspective, shift the narrative, and change the story.

pivot!

Give yourself permission to be flexible here. If your stories suck, change them.

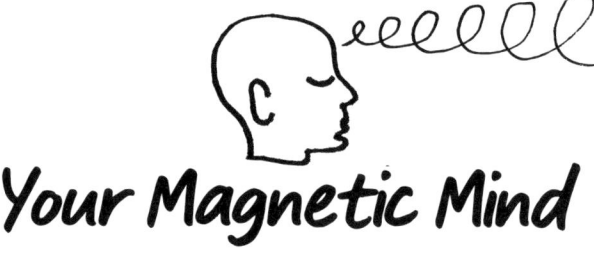

Your Magnetic Mind

I once heard someone say, *'Our brain is in our body, but our body is in our mind,'* and I felt my brain implode. The more I sat with it, the more it clicked. We usually think of the mind as something *inside* our body, when actually our body exists *within* a much larger field of consciousness. Wild, right? Let me break that down.

Your physical body is obviously the most visible, tangible layer of your energy field – the densest expression of who you are. Surrounding that are more subtle layers, each influencing your thoughts, emotions, health, and the reality you experience. Think of it as a spectrum, moving from dense to light, from matter to energy.

Here's how I understand those layers, and I'll keep it short and sweet:

- **Physical Body:** Flesh, bones, organs, the nervous system – the part of you that moves through the world. The one that sleeps, eats, and shits. You know this one well.

- **Etheric Body:** This is your life-force energy (also known as *prana, chi,* or *qi*). It's like the power grid that keeps your physical body running – an energetic template that directs energy through channels called meridians or nadis. When you recharge in nature, meditate, or rest deeply, you're chargin' up this field. Making space for play and creativity is also important here.

- **Emotional & Astral Bodies:** These layers carry your feelings, desires, creative impulses, wounds, triggers, and lived experiences. When emotions get activated, stuck or suppressed, they can enhance or distort your field and influence what you attract (it brings the good shit and the bad). The Astral is more focused on subtleties and imagination, but I believe there is an overlap with the felt-sense of the Emotional Body.

- **Mental Body:** You guessed it. All your thoughts, beliefs, and stories hang out here – both the ones you've created and the ones you've inherited. A cluttered mental body sends out mixed messages to the Universe, so clean shit up.

- **Causal or Spiritual Body:** Kinda like the driver's seat; your higher mind, intuition, and soul memory. This is where patterns, lessons, and karmic imprints live – the codes around what you're here to experience.

- **Etheric Template Body:** Think of this as your *original design* – a perfect, untampered energetic blueprint of who you truly are and what's possible for you. It's pure potential, untouched by fear, limitation, or distortion. It's like a hologram your body is built from.

- **Celestial Body:** The realm of higher love, compassion, and joy. When you feel a deep sense of connection, forgiveness, or unity, you're tuning into this layer. Nice, eh?

- **Ketheric (Causal) Body:** The outermost layer of your energy field, where your individuality dissolves into pure Source consciousness. Kinda like the web that's attached to everything. The term 'kether' comes from the Kabbalistic Tree of Life and represents unity with divine awareness.

Each of these bodies interacts with the others. A disruption in one layer ripples through the rest until it eventually shows up in your physical reality – fatigue, illness, emotional chaos, or repeating life patterns are just the body's way of showing us where the energy is out of balance. Everything is connected, and when you begin to understand these layers, you start to see how your energetic state shapes your lived experience.

 Your mind and heart are constantly broadcasting through your energetic field, working like a transmitter and receiver. Your mind sends out thoughts – signals to the Universe – and your heart (with your emotions) acts as the magnet that draws experiences back in. Imagine all of that happening around your little human body. You're like a fountain of ever-flowing energy. So, yea, I guess your human body really is in your mind *yes,* (and so much more). You're kinda like a sexy lasagna, layered up, lookin' *you're* saucy and bossy, all cute 'n shit. *a spiritual lasagna*

And in the center of granny's favorite lil' lasagna is your big, gorgeous heart generating what's called a toroidal field (see opposite) – a flowing doughnut-shaped energy field that moves out from your body and circles back up and in again. It's heavily influenced by your emotions *(energy in motion, see page 52)*, and it plays a huge role in the life you're co-creating.

Together, your thoughts send the signal, your emotions power the field, and your reality takes shape accordingly. The Universe doesn't judge, it just mirrors what you're emitting. *As within, so without.*

So, if your Etheric Body is depleted because you're not resting, not recharging, not protecting your energy, your field weakens. If your Emotional Body is clogged with unprocessed pain, fear or trauma, your toroidal field sends out mixed frequencies – one minute love, the next minute scarcity or mistrust. If your Mental Body is full of limiting beliefs, or your ex-lover who's honestly a bit of an asshole, then those thoughts create more stories, those stories trigger more erratic emotions, and those emotions attract more of the same erratic expression externally.

Coherence is key.

Toroidal Field (Basic)

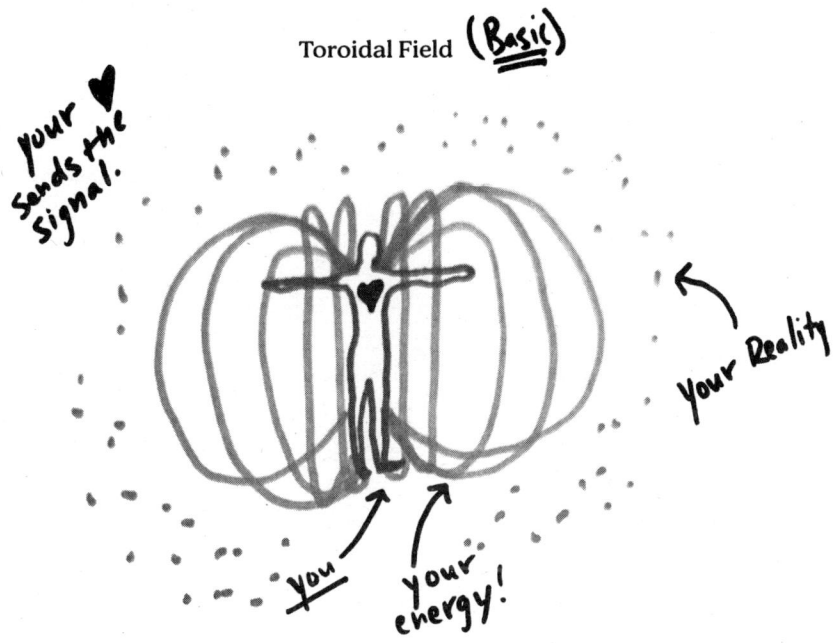

your heart sends the signal.

your Reality

you

your energy!

This is why energetic self-awareness matters. Healing isn't just about your physical body; it's about tending to the unseen architecture that shapes it.

If you strengthen your Etheric Body, clarify your thoughts, and process your emotions, your energy becomes coherent. Your field becomes magnetic. Your life starts to align with what you truly want, not what your old distortions are projecting.

So, experiment with this. Tune into your layers. Feel it all. Notice what feels heavy or drained, what feels open or light. Because when your mind, heart, and all your bodies are in harmony, your field becomes magnetic, and you don't have to chase what you want – your desires start to move toward *you*.

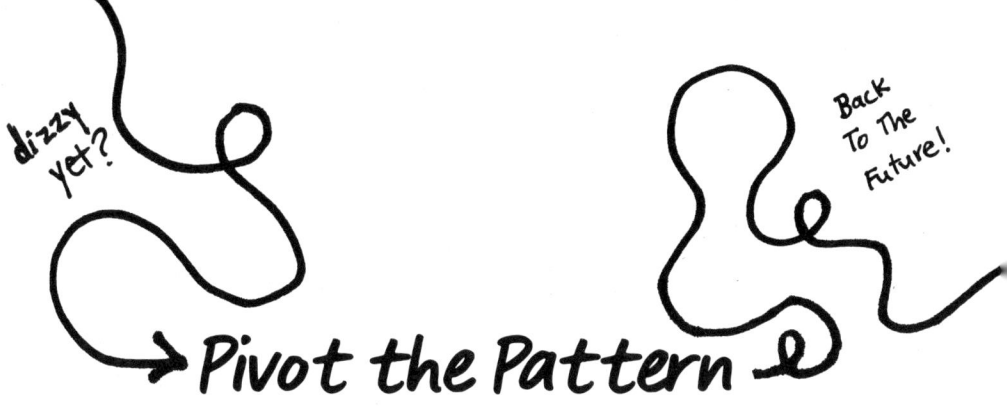

Pivot the Pattern

dizzy yet?

Back To The Future!

That was a ride! Now, flip me up the 'right way up' and turn to page 71.

Jump forward to page 70

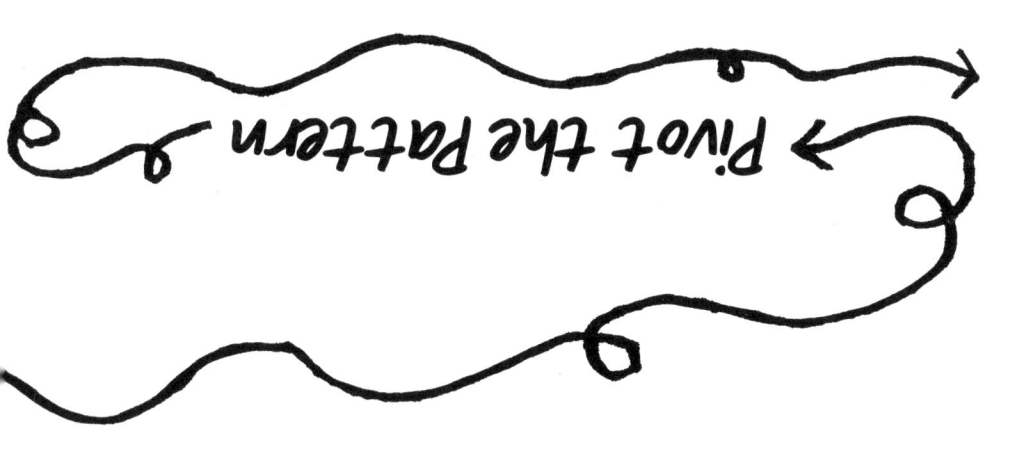

Pivot the Pattern

call move through what is most alive first – in this case Fearful Freddy – and then I intentionally call in someone who can help me recalibrate into the opposite emotion, in this case Trustworthy Tim. I write it down. I burn it. I shake my booty. I hug myself. And I get off the call and back to life. Sometimes it takes five minutes, sometimes it takes 45 minutes, but the shift happens. Experiment with it.

This feels like an appropriate time to mention, we don't always need to understand the root of everything. You'll drive yourself fuckin' crazy trying to make sense of it all. Just move the energy as best you can.

Name your emotions.

Have a conference call.

Give them some space to share.

And move on when you feel better.

Keep in mind: The more ridiculous the names, the better. Laugh at them. Play with them. Let them freak the fuck out. Then call in your crew to help recalibrate. Have fun with it.

Take a peek!

from our family, or religion, etc. but they can be altered and adjusted with patience, practice, and time. So now when Fearful Freddy shows up, I sit with him. I feel fear *(see Pause With the Panic on page 44)*. I literally say, out loud, 'Ok, Freddy what's up? What do you need right now?' Trust me, Freddy will GO OFF. I let him spiral and ruminate and have a full fucking meltdown about all the ways I'm dying and why everything is falling apart, and everything's failing, and then when he's done, I say, 'Anything else?' And then boom, Freddy is on a roll again. And when he's done, I'll ask again, 'Anything else?' I keep this up until he has nothing left to say. We have spiraled and landed at rock bottom. Thank God. Sometimes I'll even write down Freddy's rants and then burn the paper it's written on (safely).

By acknowledging Freddy and all his fears I can witness the energy and help it move. I don't get caught in the story. I don't respond or try to alter it – I let the energy, the emotions, the feelings, the stories come up as they are without trying to alter them. I let the energy be what it is, without judgment or manipulation, and I let it move out of me. I have a good laugh at how ridiculous some of it is, and I honor what feels real and terrifying. Then, I interrupt the patterning and start to architect a new archetype. Enter Trustworthy Tim. And Healthy Harry. Tim knows we've got this. He knows I'm good. He trusts the flow. After Freddy's little meltdown, Tim cleans shit up. Healthy Harry recalibrates my field. I have intentionally built Trusty Tim and Healthy Harry to step forward and align me with the energies I want to experience. They help me anchor the energy into my field. I somatically move my body. I jump, dance, breathe, and laugh. I change my state. I acknowledge and alchemize pain into feelings of trust, health, and happiness. I work with Tim to say, 'I am safe. I am okay. I am protected. I trust my process. I've survived up until now, I'll survive this too.' I work with Healthy Harry to say, 'My body is whole. My mind is clear. I can trust my body to take care of itself. It is intelligent. My energy is balanced. I am safe.' I let everyone have their moment. I let the conference and see how you feel. I mean, you're already reading upside down. Look at you go! All twisty & turvy. Why not try something else?

Conference Calls

Repetitive thoughts are flags that we need to move this energy and return to a centered state. One way to interrupt these repetitive thoughts and loops is by having what I call a conference call. We give our ideas and internal voices a character, we sit them the fuck down, and we help them chill out for a minute. The first step is to recognize the thoughts and voices. Give them a name. Then give them space to share their thoughts. It's up to us to hear them out. After we hear them out, we can begin to architect new archetypes to balance out the energy, or at least work with these archetypes in a meaningful way. Those voices just want to be heard. They want to be seen. A simple acknowledgement of what's alive will help shift your experience. Don't be afraid of them, let them speak.

Fearful Freddy shows up often for me. He wants to freak out when something goes awry. He tries to convince me that everything's going to fail or that I'm dying (dying rears up a lot for me). When part of your ego is dying off, your body senses the energetic or psychological death and transition and oftentimes interprets that doomsday 'I'm dying' feeling with the fear of literal death, when in reality you're just shifting energetically. Judge Judy likes to show up for me too. She makes fun of people, or interrupts me to make a judgment call when I'm trying to pay attention to someone because she thinks I know better or will discount what they're saying entirely because they have a sesame seed still stuck in their teeth from their breakfast bagel and schmear.

 important

The voices in my head, these emotions, feelings, stories, and beliefs, they're not all mine, but they are my responsibility to manage. Most of them come from society, or our conditioning, or what we learned or inherited

you continue doing everything the same... that's one definition of crazy, no? Doing the same thing over and over again and expecting a different outcome? At the very least, I drove myself crazy doing that for weeks, months, sometimes years at a time. And then I started walking backwards. Yes, literally. For like five or ten minutes in the morning, or sometimes I would put on a song and just walk with the song through my apartment, backyard, bedroom... wherever I could walk, I would walk. Backwards. Sometimes I would just start crying out of nowhere while walking backwards – it was like my body could feel the change happening and there would be a cathartic somatic release. Amazing. That's the goal – change!

You can take this same thing and apply it to driving to work. No, not driving backwards, but taking a new route. Take the scenic route, take a different road, take the long way! Change your bus or train. Intentionally travel differently, even if it takes a bit longer. Just do what you can to not go the same way you always go. Why? Because I said so. Also, because your brain is literally forced out of autopilot. Your brain begins to activate and use different neural pathways – that means new ideas, thoughts, and solutions. These simple actions begin to stimulate neuroplasticity and that is a recipe for new learning, better memory, and new behavioral thoughts and patterns. These new routes challenge your brain's executive functioning and allow you to adapt more easily to change and breaking out of rigid habits, thoughts, or stories that overtime we get stuck in. Break the loop!

Walking backwards is not only opening new mental channels but the practice of physically moving backwards is demanding multiple regions of the brain to work together. Your balance, your spatial awareness, your coordination, and the cross communication of all these parts enhances the part of our brain that supports self-regulation and decision-making, inviting in easier shifts in our everyday life. Trust me, it might feel weird. Great. Weird is good. Go be weird. Go walk backwards. Let's flip the script for a minute and see what happens. Experiment with it for a few weeks

A similar pattern happens when we are stressing about the future – our mind is trying to prepare us for the worst-case scenario so it doesn't hurt so bad later. The issue is that this perception is experienced the same way in the body as if it's happening right now. Our nervous system doesn't know the difference between past, present, and future. It can't identify what's happening now, has already happened, or what we think will happen in the future. Our nervous system is responding as if it's real, right now. The more we focus on the worst possible outcome, the more our neural pathways fire and the neuroplasticity in our brain tags this repetitive thought as important, because it keeps coming up. Now, we shape our mind to see things this way, and we keep the momentum going. We anchor into these stories. These stories make us believe certain things. These beliefs make us feel some type of way, and because of these feelings we make certain choices. Those choices often result in outcomes and experiences that reinforce the feelings, beliefs, and stories, and there you have it – we're caught in another loop.

The Loop: Stories → Beliefs → Feelings → Choices → Stories

this shit helps! Walking Backwards

Walking backwards is one of my fave ways to repattern. The importance of shifting our reality and our patterning can really only be amplified by physically changing things up. Imagine, you want a different outcome but

Welcome!

Flip you

it!

Well, that shook you up and upset your programming! This chapter is all about shifting your perspective, challenging your preconceptions, and reshaping your reality, so it only seemed appropriate to flip this book on its head.

Now, let's think about what goes on in your head. Have you ever been through a break-up and you keep going over every tiny detail of how it all fell apart? Or do you keep having the same fight in your head with someone who pissed you off? There's a reason we get caught in rumination and/or fear-based thinking. Our prefrontal cortex is wired to problem solve and our ego is trying to make sense of a situation to create an experience of safety. If we can't control an outcome our mind will ruminate to create a false sense of control. Our nervous system can get hijacked by this experience, making us feel emotionally and physically anxious or unwell. Half the time this isn't even conscious, it's moving under the surface creating an overall sense of unease and dissonance that we can't quite name.

The problem is that our Default Mode Network (DMN) and our limbic system create a repetitive thought pattern (overthinking) in an attempt to resolve a perceived threat, or unprocessed emotion or story. Our amygdala, the fear center, begins to tag certain thoughts and memories with emotional intensity when we're in a state of fight or flight, because it's perceiving what feels like a very real threat. If we don't have closure, or we can't make sense of a situation from the past, our mind ruminates on it trying to find any possible solution, or outcome, so that we can close the loop and return to safety.

Now flip this the right way round

Triggers and Flags (Pain Points)

Triggers are your best friends. Learn to love them. They're usually the first sign that something is unhealed, unprocessed, or unresolved. The audacity of a trigger to make you feel a particular way and seemingly out of nowhere! Honestly, what a gift. When we're triggered, we're dysregulated. We get upset, we start to sweat, our stomach drops, or we feel a sense of contraction as our body attempts to communicate with us *(see The Body Is Technology on page 35)*. Maybe your partner is late and you're triggered thinking they're out cheating. Maybe your mom tells you to change your shirt and you feel immediately enraged, like you have no agency or she's always judging you. These aren't just triggers. They're teachers. These pain points are portals for change.

Everything in life is material for our growth. There's literally a tree growing on Anna's roof *(read about Gloria on page 134)*. Anna's one of my best friends who's helping me write this book, and she's an Aries so she's super familiar with triggering the shit out of people (I love you, Anna). That's also why I love Aries energy in general: they don't give a shit what other people think and it's so funny to see what that triggers in people – joy, shock, anger... what a gift! Anyways, back to Gloria, the tree growing out of her shingles. She's literally growing out of nothing! A bird must've shat a seed onto her roof and this lil' fucker still figured out a way to rise to the occasion. It used its turbulent environment to grow and bloom and still become something beautiful. So, what's your excuse? We've all been through some shit that, in hindsight, helped us create something beautiful, right? So maybe you're a tree blooming on the roof right now, amazing! Maybe you're not, and that's also fine. But if you find yourself on a white, creamy, downward spiral, toward a rock bottom that looks like a terracotta roof shingle, please keep in mind: This shit could be the soil you need to bloom into the beautiful being you're on your way to becoming. Let Gloria lead by example.

Alright, back to triggers. I want you to begin to flag these moments of flaring up with rage, or sadness, or feeling like you can't trust someone, and investigate the story beyond the reaction. Your reaction is revealing that there's something deeply rooted in you that still needs love, forgiveness, care, understanding, and/or attention. This connects to the idea of mirroring *(see page 144)*. When we have these 'Ouch' moments we can begin to understand ourselves on a deeper level. They show us where we need to do some work; they serve as our emotional compass or internal GPS device, and again, it's already wired into our bodies.

That's the technology. Use it to your benefit and instead of flipping the table and slapping someone across the face, work with it. Create a little more space to acknowledge there's something under the surface that needs your attention. Thank your emotions for guiding you there. Be grateful a coworker pushed that button and allowed you to see where you're still trapped. The pushed button revealed a place where you can further liberate yourself from past pain, an old story, or a perceived limitation. So, breathe. Feel fuckin' triggered and feel fuckin' blessed for it passing through. Later, when possible, dig into it, start to examine what's really going on under there, and shift it.

Here are your 'I'm triggered AF' cheat sheets. The first one is for when you want to dive deep and really begin to work through what's going on under the surface. The second list is for when you just need to get through a tricky situation. Both approaches require a little self-awareness. This is where the breathing really comes in handy; we need a small gap between 'what's happening' and our reaction to it. If you get triggered you can interrupt your innate reaction by creating a moment to breathe. You can then decide if you want to pivot the pattern in real time *(see page 64)*. You get to choose how to respond instead of being reactive. These cheat sheets can help with that as well.

'I'm Triggered AF' Deep Dive Cheat Sheet

1. **Notice the trigger.** What's active? Your mind, your body, your emotions? All three?

2. **Lose your shit.** Find a place to be alone, or with someone who can handle you losing your shit, and lose your fucking shit. Always remember: Like a fart, these energies are better out than in, so do what you can to move them. Scream. Shake. Ugly cry. Talk it out (this is where a conference call is great – *see page 67*).

3. **Now breathe.** Slow things down a bit so you can work through the layers of what's going on. Practice box breathing *(see page 41)*.

4. **Answer these questions**, preferably on paper; they sound cliché but I promise they help:

   • What is this really about? If you had to guess why you're upset, what's your first guess?

   • Simply put, how do you feel: disrespected, insulted, left out, forgotten, pissed off, humiliated, grief-stricken, jealous, etc.?

- What stories are you creating about what happened? (Not facts – the stories).

- What are you assuming about the people involved? (Don't focus on their behavior, focus on what you're assuming it means.)

- Have you felt this way before? Is this echoing another moment in your life, a repeating storyline, or experience?

Pay Attention!

- Notice your narrative: 'I'll just do it myself,' 'This always happens,' 'I'm out,' 'What did I do wrong?,' 'I shouldn't have said anything at all,' 'I'm so done with this!,' 'I deserve better,' 'Fuck them,' 'I knew they'd leave,' 'How could I compete with that?,' 'Do they know who they're talking to?,' 'Now everything's fucked up,' 'Why aren't they responding!?,' etc.? These thoughts are not truth – they're pain points revealing a thread you can pull to find something deeper.

- Have you said this before? When did a similar experience happen last? And the time before that? And before that? Trace it back to the first time a younger you went through this.

- This is where it gets good: Trace it back to your earliest memory of a similar thing happening – how old were you? What's the scene? How did you respond (fight, flight, or freeze)? What stories about yourself, the world, and the people around you were created? Here's an example: 'I don't trust that others consider my needs or desires, so

I guess they don't really matter, and that pisses me off because I feel disregarded and sad that no one gives a shit about me. If they don't care about me then I'll take care of everything myself.' This likely isn't consciously moving through your mind as a six-year-old, but in the psyche these storylines develop, and they stick until we unstick them.

5. **As you start to see it, name it.** Now when you're triggered and it comes back up, you recognize it. 'There's that story again – my abandonment spiral...' or whatever. It has less power when you notice it.

Disarm It! →

6. **Name your needs.** Behind the stories are unmet needs, find them. 'Do I need safety, validation, boundaries, certainty, connection, space, honesty, etc.?'

7. **Remind yourself, 'This is an old reaction.'** Then anchor into your desired state *(read about Anchoring on page 171)*.

8. **Unclench your jaw, shake your body, affirm that you're not crazy**, you're still cute, and you still deserve a lil' lovin'. 'I totally get why I felt that way.' No shame, no blame.

9. **Bridge yourself into the rewiring process** – 'I see the pattern – I'm choosing to pivot'

10. **Pivot.** Other chapters will help you pivot the patterns and rewire yourself, that's the other half of this work. The first part is identifying the shadows that were previously running the show.

There it is, now you'll never be triggered again. Congrats! You're healed, fully and forever. Fire your therapist and start charging people $1,111 for Light Language Alignment Activations so you can help others transcend as well. And make sure you buy a big hat and body jewelry. You can use the rest of the pages in this book to wipe your client's tears, or your own ass or whatever, because with a hat like that, you won't need me!

I'll still drop the second cheat sheet here in case one of your new clients needs it. It's great for when your drunk uncle is pissing you off at your aunty's birthday and you just need to get through dinner without punching someone in the throat:

'I'm Triggered AF' Simple Cheat Sheet

1. Get triggered – probably the easiest part.

2. Breathe and calm down.

3. Consider the consequences of flipping the table, or other possible over-reactions.

4. Choose peace over punching.

5. Pivot the conversation and redirect your energy to something else or remove yourself entirely.

6. Open your Notes app and write down what happened, how you felt, and dive deeper later (on page 73).

For Family, Dinners, + Dates.

I guess that's really it.

Triggers shows us where misalignment exists. The frustrations, friction, or our desire for something more – these are hints that the self and the soul are not aligned. Triggers help us identify where we're stuck so we can unstick ourselves.

Less Triggers = Less Stickiness

Less stickiness = More Flow

Indifference is often an indication that you're at peace. When you see your ex and feel neutral. Or when you receive harsh feedback and feel okay with it. I'm not talking about apathy, I'm talking about acceptance. From a place of neutrality, we can weave love back into the experience and return to appreciation and gratitude. Now we're dancing with life again. It's a process. Simple, but not easy. And trust me, I wanna flip a table too sometimes. I get it. But we're here to dance, not to flip tables. We're here to enjoy life and all the good shit, but we're also here to learn. Paying attention to triggers helps us map out the path of our growth, and like most things in the subconscious, they're more dangerous when they're unknowingly active. Experiment with some of the practices on these cheat sheets to create a little distance between your triggers and your reactions. This is how we really change things; imagine each trigger as a fork in the road – do we cycle back into the same reaction, or do we choose how to respond? Your choice.

Now, trigger this QR code

Disappointment (ft. Ariana Grande)

let us be grateful

Disappointment arrives when your reality doesn't match the picture in your head. The text that never comes. The job you almost got. The apartment that goes to someone else. The trip that gets cancelled at the last minute. It can be petty, it can be profound, but, as always, it's data.

My relationship with disappointment has evolved over the years and now I see it as the teacher and guide it really is. Disappointment shows us what we want; what we truly desire. It also shows us how we react, and what is most alive within us when we don't get what it is we think we want. Disappointment triggers emotions, stories, and feelings that dwell beneath the surface. It brings to light what it needs to, so we can set ourselves free from the deeper beliefs and ideas that keep us unconsciously stuck. It's not always a pleasant experience, but if we can play with shifting our lens from disappointment to understanding what is being triggered, it can be a very potent medicine. Work with it as best you can.

Disappointment struck while I was writing this book, and on the surface, it probably sounds *super petty* – but it actually taught me a lot about myself, because I managed to stop and take stock of what was going on for me beneath the surface. I had booked myself into an incredible 5-star hotel, the Torel Palace, a 19th-century beauty built as a symbol of wealth and Porto's Romantic era. I wanted to sit in this aristocratic mansion and work on my book. I had my whole weekend mapped out: museums, inspiring new environments, and a luxury stay to really unplug, unwind, and unburden myself from the everyday bullshit we all move through sometimes. But the Universe had something else in mind. A real kick in the ass. On my drive to the hotel, I called to ask if I could schedule a massage, and to my unpleasant surprise they explained there had been a flood in my room and that they had to move me to their sister hotel, Saboaria, which loosely translates to... soap factory (and definitely does not loosely translate to Palace).

Now, Saboaria is another 5-star hotel, but *soap factory* didn't quite have the ring to it that *palace* did. Hesitant, but without options, I accepted the pivot and they said they would upgrade me to a better room and treat me to a free massage. At first, I was annoyed, then I chose to lean into excitement. I did a little gratitude dance, and 52 minutes later I arrived.

Then things went south. Not because this hotel wasn't stunning, and not because of the generous upgrades... but because this whole experience was triggering the shit out of me. (*Read about Triggers on page 71.*) My subconscious, my fears, my need for control did not approve. Cue the panic. *This wasn't my plan. Loss of control = loss of safety. Uh Oh!* Everything they tried to do to help, I weirdly rejected. The freebies they offered... *What strings are attached!?* Every time they opened a door or said 'Mr. Corsini,' I cringed or got a chill up my spine. I found myself walking around with an ungrateful smirk that likely got me labeled as the 'spoiled brat in Room 28.'

I could also see myself being overly expressive about my dissatisfaction. It was like when my friend Vials dropped her phone off the side of the boat while we filmed a killer TikTok — I saw it happening but couldn't stop it. I'm so self-aware that it felt like I was sitting in a movie theater watching a montage of my worst moments. Then the guilt set in. *I'm in a five-star hotel and I can't just enjoy it? WTF is wrong with me!?* Cue the shame spiral.

So, what was really going on?

The problem was my wiring – the trauma response, fear-based thinking, and certain influences from my past. What actually happened when the plan changed was that all of my old shit came up. When something changes unexpectedly my nervous system says, 'I'm not safe unless I take control!' Instead of actively engaging in my needs and expressing them clearly, I became passive aggressive. Another outdated reaction rooted in my fear of speaking up for myself.

In the past there were times when gifts were given but they came with certain conditions or invisible strings attached. I've been told once or twice, 'You're so ungrateful for everything. Look at all that I've done for you.' Whether it was true or not, it created some kind of narrative in my mind. Am I ungrateful? Is a gift only a gift if you're kissing the feet of the gift giver? Both of these experiences – the massage, the upgrade – it activated a 'strings attached' narrative for me that is wired into an outdated imprint. It's like part of me believes that some things come with a hidden cost, or that at some point they will be held over me as a point of shame or guilt or manipulation... causing me to feel suspicious about the offer of the free massage – how free is it? The smiles from the hotel staff or every time they opened a door for me. Did they really mean it? My hyper-vigilance was activated as my brain began to scan the environment looking at everything that was going wrong instead of what was going right.

Coming from a bit of a turbulent childhood, being in control was one way of securing a sense of safety. I was pulled back into this survival technique, and whatever they gave me felt weirdly wrong, like I was waiting for the other shoe to drop, and part of me was thinking *I need to get TF out of here.* Of course, that's not the conscious narrative in my mind when I get triggered in this way, but there's an unnerving feeling that certainly stems from that idea. If something were held over me in my younger years, the shame and guilt would set in. I would give myself a hard time for being wrong, or selfish, or bad. I'd feel insecure that I was unable to provide myself with those things and that I needed to rely on someone else. I felt shame and self-loathing that I couldn't give back the same value I was receiving. Or that they could see something I couldn't, that I'm defective or fucked up because I'm selfish and not grateful. Those were the stories in my mind and they felt very real, even if they weren't. I'm not saying it was done on purpose, but that's how I felt, and those things helped shape an understanding of myself and others, even if it's false. So now to avoid those feelings, I unconsciously interrupt my ability to receive in the first place. This creates an inner conflict between the part of me that needs to receive and the part of me that ties receptivity to weakness or manipulation. I've seen this show up in many relationships and it was a common thread for years until the pattern became conscious. It wasn't a nice thing to see about myself, but I was able to understand that behind the disappointment, somewhere deep in my subconscious mind, there was still a story that I am ungrateful, selfish, or unable to provide for myself or others. The common thread between these three themes is an understanding that I was not enough. And just like that, the disappointment brought me into another layer of awareness of myself – completely unrelated to the soap factory or the palace hotel, but insanely beneficial for me to discover.

I'd been here many times before, but this time was different. I chose to interrupt the pattern and began to see what was happening in a whole new way. I noticed a few things: Firstly, it was okay that I felt disappointed. Yes, it was a trivial thing in the grand scheme of things, but I had been really excited about the specific experience I had booked... I wanted to be the prince of the palace, not hanging out in a soap factory (even if it was beautiful)!

lol K
grow up!

Secondly, instead of communicating my discomfort, or clearly advocating for my needs, I was displaying disappointment by moping around, and rolling my eyes in a passive aggressive, indirect way to communicate what I was feeling. I was subconsciously hoping that someone would notice and feel inspired to ask me what they could do to help. Then when they *tried* to help, I felt irked because it felt inauthentic. Basically, I was being emotionally manipulative. I presented a 'woe is me, help me, help me' energy instead of speaking the fuck up and saying, 'THIS IS WHAT I NEED PLEASE.' Maybe in the past I felt overlooked until I was sad, or injured, or upset. This pattern revealed those tactics. It also revealed how I often suspect there's a hidden motive, fine print, or an invisible price tag attached to things.

Disappointment shows up for good reason. It shows us that we want more for ourselves, it acts like a compass helping us see where things aren't matching our heart's desires, it's a push forward and invites us to try again or to understand something deeper about ourselves. It's an invitation to deeper wisdom; it acts like a mirror to show us where we're at and where we can go next.

Disappointment reveals how we cope, how we react, how we manage ourselves through the act of not getting what we think we want. Disappointment can expose our strategy, it can reveal the underlying narratives that we have about ourselves, if we're truly willing to see them. It presents our patterns and deeper wiring to us and helps us understand how we manage or manipulate the situation (or others) into helping us get what we want. Even if we're unaware of it. Find yourself rolling your eyes? Communicate your frustration – speak up for yourself. Are you huffing and puffing like you're gonna blow that little piggy's house right down? Ask directly for what you want. Maybe when you grew up, it didn't feel safe to express yourself, or your needs weren't being met. You can change that now. But that change requires your voice. So, speak up, you deserve to be heard, and your needs matter.

None of this is meant for you to beat yourself up over; in fact it's meant to empower you so you *can* get what you want, but in a direct way, with integrity. Disappointment offers us a choice: Do we ride out our old patterning or do we advocate for ourselves? Do we practice gratitude for the things we have, honor ourselves in the moment and clearly communicate our needs, expectations, hopes, and desires? Or do we huff and puff?

When we show up in truth, others can too. We invite others into a positive collaboration when we act in integrity. When we present ourselves honestly everyone can actively participate in finding solutions; I've found the more honest I show up the more willing people are to actually help. And the faster you can understand who is truly aligned with you. You'll find out sooner where people are at, and you can adjust yourself accordingly.

Disappointment finds us in many places, at various times, throughout our life. It shows us our patterning and desires around what we really want from relationships, work, expression, and more. What I'm realizing now is that it's important for me to recognize the unconscious parts of myself that affect all my relationships and continue to hinder my experience of love and joy and expansion. Disappointment triggers our edges, our comfort zone — it reveals where we're still trapped. Disappointment directs us toward what we truly desire by first helping us see what we need to detox. Disappointment is part of the divine design to help us liberate ourselves. What's really going on beneath the surface when your disappointment hits? Witness it. Explore it. Experiment with it.

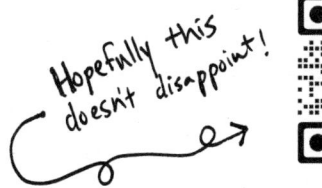

Hopefully this doesn't disappoint!

okay, it's story time

Ariana Grande disappointed me once. Yes, that is, our paths did cross. She unfollowed me on Instagram and my gay little heart broke. She had followed me a year or two earlier and I freaked out. How could you not? She's a gay icon. Then one day, I got a request to work one-on-one with some of the big wigs from the Hollywood adaptation of the hit Broadway musical *Wicked* and for whatever reason I decided to check up on Miss Galinda herself, and I noticed that she was no longer following me. She literally said 'Thank You, Next' and floated off in a little pink bubble. Maybe her monthly tarot forecast hit just a little too close to home or something, or maybe her time with me was just up; that happens. I heard it said that people come into our lives for a reason, and then we move on. Either way, Ari, it's fine. It's totally cool. I'm not upset. And I forgive you for the single dramatic tear I did shed. It may well be that we will never meet again in this lifetime, so let me say before we part, I did see *Wicked* six times in theaters despite our breakup (I also saw it nine times on Broadway but who's counting?). And Glinda, just know, I see you – you blew my mind with that role. And that Golden Globe nomination you got fuckin' robbed of!? Don't even get me started on that or the Oscars, okay? Anyways, I'm glad I laid that to rest. I miss you. And I have been changed for good.

Ariana Grande unfollowed me :'(lol

Demons and Dragons

Let's start by clearing the air around the word demon. It comes from the Greek word *daimon*, which means spirit, divine power, or guiding force. Not evil. Just energy. Later, Christian theology twisted *daimon* into 'demon,' loading it with fear and darkness. But at its root, a demon is simply an energetic current moving through you.

Think of this current as the wind guiding a sailboat. You're the captain. The sails catch the wind, and you choose how to steer. How you harness that wind, and which direction you let it pull you, is down to your free will. The wind isn't good or bad. It can feel strong or weak, rough or gentle – but what matters is how you work with it. Our demons are currents of energy, and it's how we harness them that really matters.

I'm going to help you look at those demons – those energies, those guiding forces – directly in the eyes, so you can see them for what they are and decide where you want that wind in your sails to guide you. Some of these energies are beautiful and expansive. Some keep us stuck. But it's how we respond that counts.

Now imagine those currents as dragons. *E-motion is energy in motion (see page 52)*. Every feeling is a demon. Every demon is a dragon. And you are Khaleesi from *Game of Thrones* – the Dragon Mama. Yes, you are the Mother of Dragons, the Breaker of Chains, The Unburnt, the Queen of Meereen, the Rightful Heir to the Iron Throne. You found those eggs, and now you've got a whole motherfuckin' den of dragons inside you, waiting to be acknowledged, guided, maybe even tamed. Let's light this shit up.

You get to choose which dragons you let loose. Maybe it's the Dragon of Joy, the Dragon of Creativity, the Dragon of Desire. Maybe you keep the Dragon of Rage on a shorter leash, or learn to soothe the Dragon of Envy. Some dragons you ride all the way into a sunset of play and possibility. Others you hold, manage, or redirect so they don't burn everything down.

And some dragons just need balance. Maybe you dial down the Party Monster Dragon so you can ride the Sunday Morning Wellness Dragon and recharge. Maybe not. Your dragons. Your choice.

When those dragons rear their heads – or that daemon moves through you – pause long enough to notice. Only then can you decide: Do I ride this dragon? Do I not? Do I redirect its fire somewhere productive or do I just blow this shit up?

Who's to say?

But your dragons aren't here to destroy you. They're here to show you what's alive. Some are louder than others, so always remember: You are the Mother of Dragons, and you have the power – 'Dracarys!' I'm pretty sure that command means 'unleash fire,' so maybe start with a different dragon.

Shadow Work

Carl Jung, a Swiss psychologist and psychiatrist (I'm sure you've heard of him), first came up with the shadow idea to refer to the parts of ourselves that we hide or avoid looking at. It can include both feelings and experiences we left unnamed or even 'buried.' Some of them are conscious, others are not. And those are the ones you should be afraid of. Like little monsters lurking under your bed, our unconscious shadows are ready to stop us experiencing joy, trust, play, and expansion. They don't want us to leave our comfort zone because that can be scary. So here they come. Kicking and screaming when we're in a moment of vulnerability. One trigger after another.

These shadow elements aren't just formed in our early childhood, they're also learned behaviors, coping mechanisms, and stories that stem from wounds, trauma, and difficult unprocessed shit we swept under the rug long ago or at a time when we didn't have the resources or knowledge to manage it. Our shadow aspects keep us stuck in mental loops, rumination, and fear-based thinking. When we shine a light on them, we can work with their energies instead of letting them run the fucking show. The goal of shadow work isn't to get rid of these hidden aspects, or to ban them and cast them away, but to bring them into consciousness and integrate them into who we are.

It feels a bit foreign to feel fully accepted when you grew up the way I did. That may come as a bit of a surprise to some people, but my nervous system is fucking shot, folks. I was often othered in school. I was bullied. I became the class clown – in part to control people and have them laughing with me instead of at me. I grew up gay (still am, just checked). My parents divorced at a young age. My college years were addiction prone and sexually traumatic. A few heavy traumas in childhood, teen years, again in college. Issues with lying and cheating partners. The list goes on. Even today I can easily fall back into fear based on something somebody says or does. People can show me again and again that I'm safe with them, then something happens, BOOM – I can easily revert to my old thought patterns, reactions, and stories that are rooted in danger, abandonment, or the fear of being seen. But at least I see them. So, they don't run the show. That's more than most people can say.

These shadows want to keep us in survival; they drag our ass back into unhealed reactions and behaviors. For example, I fall into people-pleasing. Performance over the purity of who I am. Rejecting what I want, or truly desire, for acceptance and safety.

My most recent relationship helped rewrite a lot of my old programming. I was really doing the work. I would get triggered as shit, I would experience the whole meltdown internally, but I wouldn't impulsively react. I wouldn't do anything destructive. I would literally just sit with myself until it passed. I saw my shadow parts, worked with them, and I chose a different response. Over time, this helped me to repattern my nervous system, reshape my mind, and reorganize my responses and actions. These triggers were pointing at pieces of myself that remained overlooked or still active. Our shadow elements bring into the light what needs to be cleared.

So, when was the last time you met one of the monsters under your bed?

What did they do?

What stories did they tell you about yourself?

Yours are different from mine, but we can ask the same questions to begin uncovering them.

Time to bust out the journal.

Put It on Paper

There's no 'right' way to journal. Just pick up a pen and write. Your only concern should be picking a method that's sustainable. Maybe it's banging on the typewriter for an hour each morning while you drink your coffee. Or you light a candle, put on some music, and get super cozy. Maybe you sit in a park and dictate into your Notes app. The point is to get your thoughts and feelings out of the body. Stop keeping them bottled up inside or one day you're gonna pop, seriously.

If you want, turn journaling into a ritual. Choose a time, choose a place, be intentional. Your spirit guides like consistency so if you show up at the same time every day you'll build a rhythm with them, and it'll help deepen your connection and build energetic momentum. If you can't do that for whatever reason, it's fine, but you still need to get the energy out of your body. Create space for your thoughts to be released. This energy needs to move. You can write poetry. You can write in a diary. You can write in pen, crayon, or scratch it into a potato for all I care. Just write it out. Experiment. Maybe you just want to doodle and not use words at all. Great. Paint it out, draw it out, interpretive dance it out while speaking in haiku – just get it out of your fuckin' body. Trust me, it helps.

 Writing helps you map out your mind so you can see your blind spots. Now it gets a lil' juicy:

Your experiences trigger your emotions. You brain interprets your emotions and creates a narrative about how you feel and what those emotions mean (these are your feelings , as we explored on page 58). These stories and feelings create or reinforce an existing belief system (a belief about you, others, or the world). These beliefs shape your perspective and influence your choices. Your choices create experiences that trigger your emotions and the cycle repeats.

When you put those beliefs on paper you can see them, and what you can see you can shift.

If emotions create stories, and stories are beliefs strung together in an attempt to create meaning, then surely we can shift those beliefs to create a different meaning, right? We can shift the stories we tell ourselves.

Pretend there's a 1 percent possibility that those stories aren't entirely true. Let's say your feelings are just feelings and not a clear indicator of the ultimate truth. Can you lean deeper into that 1 percent and try expanding it into 25 percent? Or 50 percent or 99 percent? Can you play with your perspective?

There's no factual 100 percent Ultimate Truth that you are the thing you think or feel you are. Even if parts of it feel true, you're allowed to change and outgrow yourself at any moment. Who you were a breath ago *Read that again.* does not limit who you can be now. But your beliefs might trick you into thinking you're something fixed rather than something malleable. You get to choose how you make sense of the situations in your life. You're already creating stories about the past; you can create different stories. What you believe about yourself is so important; it will lock you down or liberate you.

So many hidden beliefs remain in our shadows. That's why they're called 'shadows' – they're lurking somewhere beyond our consciousness. After something comes to light, if we're aware of it and we're still doing it, it's a choice. It's no longer a shadow – you're aware, and you're choosing it. That means you can choose something else. Sometimes these shadows and beliefs are inherited from family or projected onto us by others. Shame, anxiety, regret, judgment, doubt, despair, insecurity – we've all felt it. We can't stop ourselves from experiencing uncomfortable emotions, but we can shape the stories we tell ourselves about how we're feeling.

So, like they say in *Mean Girls*, 'Put it in the book!'. Get your mind out of your mind and onto paper. Start wondering why you think what you think and feel what you feel. Stop sweeping your shadows deeper under the rug and start seducing them – what do they have to say? Flirt with them a little. Invite them over for dinner. Buy some condoms in case dinner goes well. They've got all the secrets that will set you free, so grab a pen and explore them.

Let's peek @ some shadows!

I Love you.

Tell Them You Love Them

We often mistake peace for boredom; if we're conditioned into productivity then nothing happening can feel like something is wrong. This is my challenge at the moment. We might mistake sadness for weakness if we've always been praised for being strong. When our emotions were too intense as a child, or at some other point in our lives, when things get too dramatic, we sometimes just disconnect from them. We float off into a state of numbness and we stop feeling or trying to understand what we're going through as a defense mechanism to keep us safe from the pain we've been exposed to. Have you ever been falling in love with someone and you fought it? Or maybe you literally fought with them. You know when things are going too well so you need to pick a fight about some random bullshit that doesn't matter because you're more comfortable navigating chaos than stability. No? Just me? Okay.

I've been in relationships where I think I'm falling in love with someone but I'm just reconnecting to instability, loss, or manipulation. Maybe I confuse feeling good with what actually just feels familiar. Maybe I've gotten used to hypervigilance so when I meet someone who triggers that I think we're a good match. Next thing you know you find yourself in some co-dependent trauma-bond, again. You know, relationships will keep mirroring back similar experiences from the past until your psyche can either find peace with it or resolve it entirely. And then there's the relationships that actually help heal you.

My most recent relationship caused anxiety for a different reason: I felt too safe. I would get this rush through my body thinking something was wrong, but it was a complete misinterpretation. *This wasn't wrong. I was just vulnerable.* My mind would come up with different stories about why this relationship wasn't good for me. Why it won't work out. I'd scan for problems that weren't there or spiral into some toxic thought process about what he's probably hiding from me (without any evidence or reason to suggest that). This shit triggered so much panic instead of peace because love in the past felt unsafe. That's because it wasn't love.

I still have love for the man I split up with while writing this book. He unknowingly did so much to help me repattern my nervous system and reconnect with a sense of safe intimacy. I just wish that I'd told him that I love him. I cried about that for days. I never experienced an emotion like that before. This deep pit – rejecting my own love to be shared. How selfish of me? How dare I withhold what we are all here to experience? Love is the whole point, and I feel like I stole that experience from both of us. This is one of my biggest regrets.

I realized that for the first time in my life it would've been said without expectations. After 36 years I've arrived at a place where I understand the frequency of love like never before. It wasn't being weaponized by a part of me scared to lose someone. It wasn't a projection onto someone I had placed above me. It was pure, unconditional love. I'd never experienced it like that before. It unlocked something in me that I've spent years misunderstanding. And still, I withheld it out of fear of rejection or abandonment. It's only now that I realize that rejection or fear cannot survive next to love. The unconditional nature of love means that there's nothing I need back from it. True love is an outpouring of acceptance and appreciation, regardless of it coming back to you. The trapdoor of fear stole that moment from me. It stole that moment from both of us.

I've sat with this a lot and realized that whether or not the love was returned to me in that moment – which I know it would've been – didn't matter. It wasn't about what I would get in return. I wasn't saying it so they would say it back. It wasn't about what was in it for me. It was about being in love. Having love. Sharing love. That's the whole fucking point. I've thought a lot about how that moment could've healed parts of him that needed healing. I know it would've healed parts of me even deeper; liberating my fear of rejection, for one, because there was no possible way of being rejected when love comes from a place of energetic sovereignty. It was not dependent on reciprocity or request. The moment we let love truly exist, instead of being a performance for approval, it transcends rejection entirely because that level of giving can't be denied. This love was not transactional. This love was my truth. My whole truth. And how dare I deny myself of my own fucking truth. That's what really breaks my heart. Where else do I deny myself my truth? Where else do I hold myself back, or play it small, or safe, or acceptable? I weep as I type this out, knowing I did us both a disservice by withholding the love we all so deeply crave. Had I spoken up in that moment, I would've liberated every word I've ever left unsaid. I would've honored myself and spoken my truth. That's love. Self-love.

The ache I feel is not about him not hearing it – it's about me silencing my own voice.

My worst nightmare came true: My fear of rejection manifested as I rejected myself. In that moment I abandoned myself completely, and that's what hurts the most. Denying myself my truth. Another act of self-betrayal.

I can't imagine all the ways this love could've also liberated him from his own wounds, fears, and aches.

This is why love is never wasted. Regardless of the outcome, true love liberates us and taps us into truth. Rejection cannot exist there, nor fear, or heartbreak. My heartbreak was entirely self-inflicted. A heartbreak rooted in denial. I learned the hard way that withholding love hurts so much more than any fear of sharing it.

If he reads this one day, he'll know who he is.

And he will know that I love him.

Stuck

There's nothing worse than feeling like a fly stuck to that yellow sticky tape. It's like shit hits the fan (that's probably what attracted the flies in the first place), and next thing you know you hit a rut and a couple days, a month, a year speeds by and you didn't even notice.

Sometimes life keeps us stuck to help us refine ourselves. Something needs to be adjusted, fine-tuned. Or we're in a gestation period, needing to catch our breath before an incoming busy phase. Energy ebbs and flows, nothing stays stagnant forever, not unless we continue choosing to stay there.

And that's the beauty – there's always a choice. Regardless of what it is, there is always a choice to be made, and it's likely that one of those choices is a step toward liberation.

You don't have to force it, and sometimes we wanna sit in the shit for a minute, and we need to, to really feel it and learn from it, and just process whatever needs to move. That's totally fine. But at some point we need to move forward. Notice how I didn't say move on? Some things we never move on from, like losing a loved one, or the grief of heartbreak *(read about Grief on page 110)*. Regardless, we can move forward.

When there's too much input mentally, we feel stuck. We're like a buffering YouTube video – we just sit there. When we haven't processed heavy feelings, our emotional body tethers us to that moment, like we're stuck in time and space, even if we swept it under the rug and try to act like everything's okay. Our nervous system knows when we're lying to ourselves. If we don't feel safe, how could we move forward?

Experiencing what we don't want helps us to reorient ourselves toward what we do. It helps us find a new direction, but it doesn't help to obsess about it. Don't fall victim to the Drama Triangle *(see page 114)*. Don't lose yourself to endless chit chat about what's not working and how everything has turned to shit. One thing that can help unstick you is shutting the fuck up about what you *don't* want. Endless venting, drama bonding, sulking – all of this will just keep you there. If you can interrupt that urge, you can disconnect the tether. You can cut the cord to whatever is holding you back and set yourself free *(see Cord Cutting on page 122)*.

If you're feeling stuck, don't panic. You're not broken, your new life is just loading, but you could be slowing it down.

What to Do If You Feel Lost

Spoiler: You're not lost.

You're in between.

Between the past and the future, between recognition and re-shaping, between the programmed self and your creator energy, between victimhood and victory, there is something else – right now, here, where we are, the present moment.

An in-between space. A middle ground.

You've cut cords, emerged from the shadows, grieved, surrendered, and you begin again. Just know that you are safe. It might feel shaky. You haven't been here before, not like this. But <u>you survived</u> every other change up 'til now.

You're letting go of something. Maybe letting go of almost everything. Your old way of thinking. Your old way of being. Maybe a job. Maybe a relationship. The speed at which you used to race through your life. The to-do list that left no room for you to breathe. For you to check in with yourself. For you to say, I'm here, too.

If we're free-falling, our instinct is to grab hold of something. To grab on for dear life and squeeze our eyes shut. But we want to learn how to be present without doing that. We want to keep our eyes open and witness what is here and alive. We want to revel in the space of suspension. The contraction before the expansion. And there might be terror in that moment, when you let go, and you're not holding onto anything.

Can you sit in that terror?

Can you remind yourself this is a space of creation? And that you don't need to rush past it. Transition is good. Transformation is natural. Fear and excitement run on a similar feeling.

Feeling as though you're lost doesn't always feel the same. Sometimes it's confusion, overwhelm, or numbness. Maybe your nervous system has hit its max and it's a full body freak out. Your mind wants control. Your body is craving old habits. Stomach tight, breath shallow. Old patterns coming back with fears or insecurities. Maybe you're triggered AF (see Triggers and Flags on page 71).

A freak out is good. A full meltdown? Great. It blows off steam, like releasing a pressure cooker. Go. Go insane, just come back. Pause with the panic (see page 44).

Feeling lost eventually brings direction, but you can't force it. Stop hunting. The harder you chase it, the further it gets. You'll never find your way out, but you will discover it.

Discovery is rooted in curiosity and play, not control. It's about wonder, trying new things, stretching your mind to new possibilities. Not rumination. Stop marinating in misery.

Take a minute to sulk, cry it out, be annoyed, write it all down and burn the fucking paper. Then do something. Play.

You won't think your way out of this.

But you will discover something new.

Shake your fucking body!

Get outside!

Call a friend.

Name the sensation.

Rest (without guilt)

Create Something!

*Stop numbing the pain and sit with it. (it will pass)

Dance it out.

TRY SOMETHING NEW

take a nap! ZZZ

Freak TF Out for a second.

Scream in a pillow!

paint or draw something.

Feel it without trying to fix it.

Be Angry → take a kickboxing class! (Amazing if you're pissed!)

Practice Box Breathing.

Cry it out, babe.

Have an ice cream.

PART 3

THE AUDACITY TO

let go.

Nothing blooms year-round. Well, maybe a few plants like Hibiscus in the perfect environment, but babe you are not Hibiscus or Bougainvillea, and you should not expect yourself to forever be in your fullest, brightest, loudest expression. That expression changes over time, or at least it should, but it can't if you're holding on to your past for dear life, afraid of change, or worse, afraid of standing in your own power. Our power scares the shit out of us. What if we could change everything? We can, but then everything changes.

Think about some of your hardest days, or the moments you felt things were all falling apart. Moments of guilt, shame, or mistakes made that you thought you'd never survive. Think of the moments you freaked out, or yelled at someone, lied, stole, or maybe cheated another person. I hope you look back and understand that all those speed bumps helped shape you into the person you are today. Knowing what doesn't feel right helps us shape what does. I hope you find trust in these moments and understand that nothing you've been through has been wasted.

These hardships and heartbreaks sanded your edges and polished you into the beautiful being you've become.

And still, at some point you need to move forward. You need to leave the past behind; sometimes you need to shift the stories or look at things from a new perspective. Sometimes you need to let go entirely. You're not meant to carry things forever, and honestly, it takes more energy holding onto old ideas and habits than it does to surrender them. Life is transient and ever evolving. So, let's experiment with creating a little more space so we, too, can evolve.

ugh

Shame.

I grew up as a gay tap dancer who loved Polly Pockets. I was one of two boys in the dance studio. I was attending a Catholic school in a white-centric suburban town. I experienced different layers of physical, mental, and sexual abuse at times. Shame, guilt, and fear were tightly woven into my tapestry. I've cleared a lot of shame already, but like an onion, there's always another layer that'll make ya cry!

The events that cause shame might be over in seconds. We might even bounce back right away. But once shame is experienced and embodied, once our shoulders drop and we feel less than, once it's internalized, it stays. When you've eaten lunch alone in the bathroom or been bullied for dancing with the girls, shame sets in. Once you've been called a 'faggot' before you even knew what it meant, or you're forced to sit alone because you wore a green GAP sweater, that shame compounds, and calcifies, and lives with you for years to come.

It stays with your six-year-old self. It stays with you at 16. At 26. It drives your choices, it fuels addiction and other coping mechanisms, it shapes relational patterns like over-giving, over-explaining, and being overly accepting of unacceptable behavior. It has you on an endless search for connection and external validation and keeps you in performance mode. It breeds self-betrayal. Intimacy feels risky and unsettling because it exposes the parts of you that you've learned to hide because you believe that you are not enough, that being seen is unsafe, that you are unacceptable and unlovable.

Releasing shame is such an important part of our rewilding process *(read about Rewilding on page 133)*. Shame is dense, distorting, clingy, viral, and self-replicating. Shame is a fascinating emotion because unlike other emotions it rarely just passes through us, instead it sticks around and tethers us to an idea of who we are. It shapes our identity. Where guilt feels like *I did something bad*, shame tricks us into thinking *I am bad*, and that shit sticks around until we intentionally un-stick it.

I am vs. I did

Trust me on this, I grew up Catholic, and Catholics eat shame for breakfast. Well, not all of them, but some of the ones I knew loved their shame fried in the morning, not too runny, with a healthy side of judgment, and an extra-large glass of guilty projections. Shame turns the target inwards, making us blame ourselves, and keeps us stuck looping through the idea that we're faulty or fucked up. We can get so lost in the shame that we feel guilty, which creates another layer of shame, and compounds over time. Once rooted in it, we unconsciously project shame everywhere and make a fucking mess. *(Read about People and Projections on page 159.)*

Shame is such a powerful tool that it's used by some religions, schools, media outlets, marketing agencies, and other invisible structures with the intention of control. Shame can trick us into doing or buying things. It inspires censorship, both of self and others, and creates dependency. When you feel unworthy or broken, you're more likely to seek answers, validation, and approval from outside of you, likely from the systems and people who shamed you – we believe on some level that they know better and we seek their acceptance. Shame dilutes our power. A shamed person is less likely to speak up for themselves, share their ideas or insights, and they pause before taking risks, second guessing themselves out of fear of rejection or ridicule. They stop themselves from finding their own unique way and shame others for trying. Shame is a learned behavior, passed down through generations until someone breaks the cycle.

That's *you*.

Break the cycle. It's time to liberate yourself from shame altogether.

check
this out
(No shame if
you don't.)

SHAME!

Grief and Releasing

Grieving is medicine. Grief fills the empty space in our heart where we honor what once was. When we reach out to grab something we've lost, when we have nowhere to put the love we carry for something or someone we are now living without, grief steps in to help move that energy. We never entirely clear our grief, but we learn to live with it. When we have so much to give and nothing to receive it, where does that energy go? When the pain is too big to hold on our own, how do we release it? Grief helps us manage.

You're not here to play hide-and-seek with yourself. You're here to set yourself free. Love, anger, gratitude, sadness, joy, grief, resentment, acceptance, disappointment – they coexist simultaneously. So, allow all parts of you to move freely.

If that means revisiting something painful, do it. If you need support, find it. Remember the words that made your stomach drop and sit with them for as long as you need. See the face of the person who hurt you and feel that hurt. Think about the mistakes you made along the way and move the energy. You need to find a safe space to let the memories trigger whatever emotions remain unprocessed so you can move this shit out of your body. Be with it, let it move up and out. We need to feel it to heal it.

Liberate yourself.

It's not your fault you experienced that trauma, or that someone lied to you, or acted in a cruel way. None of that is your fault but it *is* yours to manage. Move through the feelings surrounding what happened so you can clear the density of it and come out the other side *(see Cutting Cords on page 122)*. We empower ourselves by creating a bit of distance here. *You* are not that trauma, or that heartbreak, or that terrible thing you once did to somebody. You played a character in the story that played out. You are not the story itself. The sooner you realize you're the storyteller, and not the story, the energy shifts. First, with acceptance. Then, with forgiveness, releasing blame, shame, and guilt. Finally, with gratitude for all the learning that came from it. We need to zoom out and understand that this experience was the catalyst for change and it helped shape you.

We don't just grieve what was, we grieve what could have been. When we leave a relationship, a job, a city, or a group of friends, we feel tons of emotions, but we don't always take time to mourn the loss of the dreams we had. All the possibilities, the fantasies, even if they were farfetched, they were ours. And now they're gone.

Sometimes the grief of what could've been is the hardest part to move through. I have an estranged relationship with my father at the moment. I often think of him, or think to myself, 'He would love this!' I pray one day things change, but for now I carry two layers of grief – the 'loss' of him, and the loss of what *could* be. It's painful to think about how much he meant to me, and I know how much I meant to him, and the support we gave each other. Our connection was unique, and exciting, deep and beautiful. I really love that man. When something amazing happens, I want to call him and let him know, but instead sometimes I'll tune into his energy and share that moment remotely with him, by myself. I meet myself in a space of tenderness for the loss of the moment we could be sharing together, and the grief I carry with that. I think about the things he taught me and send love and gratitude for our relationship, but it never fills the void.

There are so many layers of what I'm moving through simultaneously with this. Layers of love, hope, sadness, gratitude, grief, anger, possibility, loss. I'm sure you move through your own complex experiences with loved ones. All these feelings are exhausting, but it's worse not giving them space to be felt. You are where you are, so be there. The more we push things down, the more they want to come up, and the more energy they drain from us. By feeling them, we let them pass, and we reclaim our energy. Pushing them away is like having too many open tabs on your computer; it slows everything down. It's leaking your energy. We need to close the tabs as best we can. We need to feel these things through.

Be where you are...

Cutting cords can help us shift some of that energy. This is not always about clearing people away, or cutting them out of our life entirely, it's a way to recalibrate the relationship on an energetic level so we can resolve some of what's going on in the nonphysical. It may help with balancing out things in the physical, too. Sometimes that balance looks like separation, for a while or indefinitely. And with that comes relief, joy, opportunity, grief, loss, and sadness. Maybe all of it simultaneously. Either way, when we work through the denser, more complicated feelings, we create a little more space for love and understanding. We can release expectations and resistance, and we can meet ourselves where we're at.

Love will always return, eventually, but first we must feel our grief. So, grieve what needs grieving. Your past. Lost potential. Grieve a simpler time, when life didn't feel so intense or overwhelming. Grieve your old dreams and your old self. Grieve the moments you missed out on, or what you could've accomplished. Grieve what could have been. Grieve the loss of the connections – friends, family, lovers – those that left you behind. Some may return, one day, and some may not. And that's okay. As you begin to heal, you may even begin to grieve the grief itself as it begins to fade. As you let go of the stories and pain you carried for so long, you

might grieve the version of you who carried it. Grief will help liberate you from what's burdened you along the way, but it needs to be felt.

So, feel it deeply. Don't be scared. I'll be here, waiting for you on the other side.

Drama Triangle vs. Empowerment Dynamic

These two triangles shape your reality:

Drama Triangle

Empowerment Dynamic

Let's start with the Drama Triangle. You can read more about psychiatrist Stephen Karpman's work from the late 1960s, but here's the quick version. The Drama Triangle breaks down toxic relationship dynamics into three roles:

Drama

1. **Victim**: 'Woe is me.' Powerless, stuck, avoids responsibility. Often seeks advice but doesn't act on it.

2. **Rescuer**: Over-gives, sacrifices self-care, drains their own energy trying to 'save' the Victim.

3. **Persecutor**: Blames, criticizes, shames. Often rigid or controlling. Can flip into Victim mode when challenged.

These roles show up in all kinds of relationships – romantic, professional, familial. And they're not just between people; they exist within us too. You might shift between all three in one day. They're not fixed, they're transient.

Now here's the reframe.

About 40 years later, coach and author David Emerald Womeldorff introduced the Empowerment Dynamic – a similar model with much healthier roles:

1. **Creator**: Takes responsibility, acts with purpose, finds solutions.

2. **Coach**: Listens, guides, supports – but doesn't take over.

3. **Challenger**: Pushes with love. Offers truth, not criticism. Encourages learning and growth.

Power

It's not a switch you flip. You don't wake up one morning and go full Creator mode for the rest of your life. But when you spot the patterns and see where you entertain drama, you can pivot. That's the work: gently recognizing where you are and choosing to be elsewhere.

I shared this framework at my retreat and really hit a nerve. Someone pushed back hard on the term 'Victim.' They implied releasing the label diminished their trauma, that 'Victim' was the most accurate word to describe them. I get it. I've also been 'Victim' to deeply traumatic experiences that took years to unpack. Sometimes we're on the receiving end of some bullshit and fall 'victim to an outcome'. I'm not telling you to 'get over it'. That's bypassing, not healing, and we're here to metabolize and integrate our experiences so they don't become shadows swept under the rug (see Shadow Work on page 87). But we can get lost in the labels, especially if something happened in childhood. Kids can't separate themselves from stories the way adults can. They internalize blame. They become the story. We all carry beliefs that were formed in childhood – but we're not children anymore. We can choose to let go. We can shift the stories.

I'm grateful they spoke up and honored themselves (that's the whole point of this work), but it reminded me how we cling to what's familiar. Regardless of if it hurts or keeps us stuck, familiarity feels safe. Even if what's familiar is unpleasant.

Your ego will always choose a familiar hell over an unfamiliar heaven.

Your ego is wired for survival, and predictability increases our chances of that, so we stick to what we know. Even if that means navigating chaos, pain, or struggle.

Just because you almost drowned as a child doesn't mean you can't learn to swim as an adult.

Yes, what happened to you was real, and it wasn't easy.

It shaped the stories you tell yourself and the world you live in.

But don't be the story. Be the storyteller. this!

Tell yourself a story of empowerment, instead of victimhood.

When we shift the way we see things, the things we see begin to shift.

The Unraveling

Fair warning: when you start applying the practices in this book, when you set an intention to shift, purge, and pivot, everything won't stay the same. We're literally changing things. Changey means no samesies, babe. And you can't have both. You can't stack a new life on top of an old one – there's a transition period. We're restructuring our foundation. We need to deconstruct and rebuild, simultaneously. Like an overlap of timelines – the past and the future. And you're straddling the middle of it holding on for dear life. It can get murky, but the cleanse is real and the cleanse is needed.

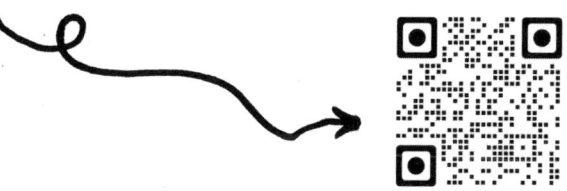

Energetic clearing also happens generationally with those willing to break the cycles they've inherited. Regardless, breakdowns support breakthroughs, and the unraveling provides space to re-weave your life more intentionally.

So why the unraveling? Old patterns, identities, and structures need to shift when you shift and the ones that don't serve your next chapter or the next version of you need to die off (or at least need new boundaries).

Imagine your new identity is emerging and the new you needs new space for new things. Everything that is not an energetic match for the new you must fall away. As we continue to grow, life will remove whatever's out of alignment with our evolving vibration, and sometimes it's abrupt. Don't dig your claws in deeper, don't hold on and squeeze even tighter – you'll make it harder on yourself. Surrender. Let go of what's being peeled away and roll with the punches. When you want more and take action, shit begins to shift. Don't cling to what was because you don't know what will be. Let go. Make available space for something new. Your energy is shifting, so is your reality. Let things dissolve – I always find they're replaced with something more aligned. Be patient. Trust the process.

When things unravel, we can feel super anxious, confused, exhausted, unmotivated, and overwhelmed, for example. Great! It's working. You're shifting. Mentally, you may spiral – old ideas, fears, bullshit coming up from your third semi-serious boyfriend who called you chubby once... I get it. But overthinking can actually be a good sign, like when you boil water and all the bubbles come up – that's you. You're like a hot pot of tea. You'll be fine, just let the bubbles up and out, and like steam they'll eventually dissolve. Surrender to what is clearing.

You're literally shifting paradigms. You're going through a birthing process in which you're both the child and the mother. And birth is fucking uncomfortable, and messy, and sometimes you shit yourself (so I've heard).

What's happening!? Why is everything changing!? – you, as the child

WTF is happening, and why is this SO uncomfortable!? – you, as the mother

Pause with the panic *(see page 44)*. Birth ain't easy, but it's beautiful. You're not dying, you're being reborn. So give yourself permission to be uncomfortable.

Shit yourself.

The Good News

SPOILER ALERT: You'll be fine, but expect a little turbulence.

Old coping mechanisms won't feel the same (especially indulgent ones like drinking, drugs, smoking, shopping, etc.).

You may question your entire identity, but you *will* prefer who you are on the other side of this.

Caterpillars also have no idea WTF is goin' on while they're becoming butterflies. I've asked, and they said it's terrifying... but they break free and soar – and so will you!

Physically, you may feel restless, experience sleep disruption, appetite changes, tension, aches or pains in the body, sudden bursts of energy and excitement, then a deep spiral into *I'M DYING!* – it's all good. I've been there. You're not dying. Your psyche is shifting, and energy is clearing; so, in some ways you *are* dying, just not physically, but your nervous system experiences it all the same. You'll be fine. Have an ice cream and chill; this too shall pass. Ride the emotional roller coaster. Put your arms up for the drop, babe. Fear into excitement, into wonder and back to worry, then loop through anxiety and pulling your fucking hair out. Welcome to what it feels like being a Gemini or a Cancer (and I'm both!). It's cool, your nervous system is recalibrating. *(Try a healthier coping mechanism on page 41).*

So why is this important?

Decay is necessary; it promotes growth. Like winter before spring. Something is on the horizon, and something's gotta give to get there. When your reality is both expanding and imploding, it's uncomfortable. It's literally clearing space for expansion.

That's all fine and dandy, and sure on paper it sounds easy enough to understand, but the experience of it can be extremely intense.

Eduardo and the Olive Tree

Imagine you're a Portuguese olive tree on my farm – you're smug, you're comfortable, you're soaking in the Mediterranean sun. Yea, you've been through changes before but you've gotten comfortable again. Then suddenly, you spot Eduardo. Every now and then this handsome young guy shows up with his rough hands, sun-kissed skin, and the stubble of a man who's too busy to shave and too dirty to care. You invite him over with a little sashay and beckoning of your branches in the breeze.

Then – BAM! Your first branch snaps and before you can gasp, he's already taking what he came for. Next thing you know, Eduardo Scissorhands is revving up his loppers, and his pruning shears are tearing off your unnecessary bits. One by one, snapped back and cut off, he hacks away everything you thought you needed. He unthreads you with his touch, spreading you open across the yard, leaving you raw and exposed to the Alentejo sun.

As heat builds and sweat drips off his brow, he's ready for another round. He pauses, waiting for a shiver of consent, which you willingly give. His calloused hands strip away your olives. With every pull on your branches, he drags a moan from your core. Without protection, you quiver on the edge of your breath. At first it feels wrong, but then it feels oh so right. You know you're safe with him. Your guard is down, and with Eduardo you journey deeper. With each thrust he pulls loose what you've held onto for years. He liberates your mind, your body, your soul.

You've done the work, you set your intentions under the Full Moon but you didn't expect change so soon. Well, here it is. Tension builds as he slaps his big wooden stick against you, shaking loose any last olives for his savory harvest. Change swells on the horizon – pressure mounting. Sensations blur between pain and pleasure. You beg for a safe word knowing it'll only ever linger on your lips.

And then it happens. He hits the spot only few can find. A point of liberation and there's no turning back. An explosive new reality lands in your lap and he finishes the job, taking more than you thought you could ever give. You both exhale. Relief, at last. He cleans himself up, and you notice you feel lighter. Taken care of. Loved. There's space to expand into something new. You're excited for your next chapter. A moment of renewal. A reset. He whispers, 'I'll be back' and you quiver for what's to come. He gets back in his truck, with his messy hair and dirty boots, and he drives off into the distance leaving a trail of dust and desire.

Eduardo will work your olives slowly until they surrender their richest oils. He'll visit you again and the thought of it alone tingles your roots. Until then, he'll taste you on his fingers, and savor your silky nectar, letting it run where it shouldn't, while you both await your next rendezvous.

And in the meantime, my dear, you will bloom like never before.

So, yea, anyways, that's pretty much how the unraveling process feels.

I hope that helps!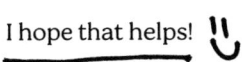

Cutting Cords

Cord Cutting is a powerful way to clear energy. It can be energy you generate or energy from other people. It can be in the form of relationships, memories, habits, beliefs, fears about the future, regrets about the past – wherever energy is leaking, whatever the story is, there's a cord there. And you can clear it, or at the very least, cleanse it.

We need to intentionally clean up our energy more frequently. It's called boundaries! Kinda like *Everyone fuck off and leave me alone*. It's not selfish, it's spiritual.

Cord cutting is great to do before reestablishing boundaries because it helps first clear shit out. Imagine cleaning your house with no garbage can, and you just pile the trash somewhere. It still stinks, yea? Take the trash out. Then set some rules about who can visit and what they can bring. That's what it's like to work with cords and boundaries. Before we establish an energetic protective layer, we want to remove all the shit, not trap it in. Clear it out. You need alone time. Divine selfishness. Protect your peace. That's the invitation. You can clear or cleanse the following energies:

- Stress, anxiety, or fears
- Toxic relationships, people, and connections
- Addictions to substances, stories, or behaviors
- Codependent people, friends, coworkers, etc.
- A struggle, story, or idea you inherited

- Limited perceptions of yourself or reality
- A bad investment (of your time, love, energy, or money)
- Bad habits or behavioral patterns
- Your controlling tendencies or people who micromanage you
- A conversation where you've been gaslit, lied to, or manipulated
- Loyalty to a family story about suffering or other unconscious agreements
- A scarcity mindset around money, health, or time
- Attachment to outcomes and stress about the future
- Rumination, obsession, or overthinking
- Past mistakes, shame, guilt, envy, or other emotions
- Any other trash you think needs to go out

Cutting a cord with someone doesn't mean you cut them out of your life (although it can). You may just be removing an unhealthy dynamic and leaving space for a healthier one. You're releasing the energetic dynamics, old feelings and stories tied to your experience. Yea, sometimes the person also needs to be taken out with the trash. If they cause a lot of issues and are unwilling to compromise, then the real test isn't recalibrating the connection, it's knowing your worth and walking away. Trust that you'll find something better elsewhere.

Because you will.

If we don't process our shit (or our parents didn't process theirs), generational trauma gets passed from one generation to the next. Even adults get triggered when confronted by defiant middle schoolers and their bossy little cliques. Maybe their unresolved high school shit comes up and they react inappropriately because they don't know how to regulate themselves. Maybe they lash out or micromanage everything else in their life to gain a sense of control. Maybe they self-soothe in toxic ways, like excessive drinking, or isolation, overeating, etc. Children who witness this behavior and think it's normal might learn these unhealthy self-soothing mechanisms and will later need to unlearn them.

Do you ever find yourself worrying like your mom? Or angry like your dad? It doesn't need to be destructive – it can also manifest as not speaking up, not standing up for yourself, or watering down your needs and pretending everything is fine just to keep the peace.

Inherited learning shapes our decisions, ideas, and actions. It shapes the way we see ourselves and the world. It keeps us playing certain roles, the roles we think are acceptable. But we can unlearn it. Start with self-compassion, see your limitations and accept that they're there, for whatever reason. No judgment, just awareness. When we create more acceptance of ourselves we can accept others a lot easier. ★

With acceptance and self-awareness, we can pivot. If you don't want to cycle through the same shit your family did, you don't have to. You can clean things up.

But you can't change what you pretend isn't there.

So, start with acceptance. Uncover any unconscious agreements and do what you can to cut or clear those cords. Liberate yourself and lead by example.

Take out the trash.

Integration

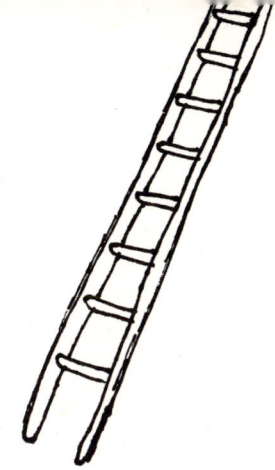

People talk about integrating our experiences as if we're downloading a new file into our old self. Perhaps we had a peak experience of some kind – a heartbreak, a mushroom trip, having a set of twins like my sister – and the idea of integration often suggests that we now need to integrate that new experience into our life. How do we fit these new pieces into our reality? Well, actually your *reality* has shifted. Maybe ever-so-slightly, maybe dramatically, but you're no longer the same person. Your consciousness has shifted, your energy field has shifted, and now reality is shifting to reflect that. Focus less on forcing the new you into your old life and instead update your old life to match the new you. It's like a staircase appeared and you're trying to drag the top floor down to the bottom. Stop moving fucking furniture and move upstairs. Don't drag everything toward you, step into the shift and match the new frequency.

You should integrate into the new vibration, not the other way around. Integration is about alignment. Finding yourself in a new vibration, a new rhythm, a new practice. You learned something? New you. Got in a fight with someone? New you. Ayahuasca ceremony? Definitely a new you. With every lesson, something shifts internally. I remember riding Puff the Magic Dragon one afternoon and BAM! It just clicked – these fears I was obsessing over were literally just a story. They were ideas that I believed, not an ultimate truth. I felt my nervous system relax and my whole body soften. I was light again, expansive. Why would I drag that energy back into my anxious little life? It's not aligned. I had a taste of the upgrade;

a snapshot of what else is available for me. I felt it in my being – a clear download of another possible reality. No fear. So, I integrated into that.

It's like life in Portugal. It's slow, laid-back, and things take time. Coming from North America I'm wired for speed. If you try to speed your way through life here, you'll just hit roadblock after roadblock. This country has its own rhythm. I need to integrate into Portugal; I can't force an entire country to integrate into my North American mindset. Integration is about new choices. New habits, practices, and environments that support us integrating deeper into a new frequency. It's not about trying to drag a new song back into your old static radio; it's about tuning your dial until you can consistently play with a new station.

let's practice

(PART FOUR)

THE AUDACITY TO
CHOOSE YOURSELF!

(crazy, right?)

xoxo

yay! ME!

It's not selfish to choose yourself, and I'm done thinking it is. We're conditioned into thinking that self-sacrifice is honorable. Sacrificing what we want is so glorified that when we set boundaries people often confuse it with rejection. So many of us prioritize other people's comfort over our own. We think going after what we want is rude or self-centered. News flash: You're at the center of your experience; you should put yourself first. Putting ourselves first often leads to guilt, so we avoid going after what we want. Society rewards people-pleasing over authenticity, so most people walk a polite road, starving themselves of their true nature.

So, what if you said 'fuck it!'?

What if you had the audacity to unapologetically put yourself first? Honoring yourself is the most important thing you can do because it aligns you with truth instead of performance. It lets you serve from a place of authenticity, doing what you want to do because you want to do it, not because you have to. No obligation. No guilt.

By choosing yourself, you become an example of what's possible for others; you inspire them to choose themselves. You cannot pour from an empty cup. You cannot give what you don't have; if you're running on fumes, you have nothing left to offer. Don't pour from your own cup. You're supposed to fill your own cup so much that it runneth over. Share only from the overpour. Share the overflow, not what's yours. Giving to yourself first makes giving to others sustainable. Like on a plane: in case of emergencies, put your mask on first before helping others. You're no good if you're passed out, head back, drooling in the window seat, babe. Put your fucking mask on.

Choosing yourself teaches self-respect and shows others how they, too, can respect you. It also shows them how to respect themselves better. When you choose yourself, you liberate yourself, and by virtue of simply doing so, you liberate others to make the same choice.

Putting yourself first isn't selfish, it's strategic — the more nourished you are, the more you can give to the world around you. Choose you.

Rewilding

The radical act of rewilding involves unlearning, deconditioning, decolonizing ourselves. Pausing in the panic instead of running from it *(see page 44)*. Rewilding returns us to who we truly are without the limits, beliefs, and programs in our mind. It invites creation from an authentic place. It means letting go of who you've been and becoming who you really are. It gives you a chance to identify, enhance, pivot, or clear certain energies. It's about aligning with your unique essence.

What bubbles up for us emotionally, mentally, even physically, helps us gather more awareness about where we are, what we believe, and what we truly desire. It helps us understand what loops we're stuck in so we can map out a new flight path. Rewilding yourself allows you to create in a way that's uniquely your own. It's about returning to self-trust. We've been taught through school, religion, and other institutions that the answers are outside of us.

They're not.

Rewilding is about connecting with your own natural cycles and rhythms. Not everything fits in a nine-to-five, Monday-to-Friday structure. Sometimes we need rest and it's not a fucking Sunday. This is about returning to your own pace, reclaiming your authentic self, and creating from there.

To get to the essence of who we are we need to first shake off everything we aren't. Shadow work *(see page 87)* and exploring how we relate to the

Four Fs *(see page 144)* help us see through any distortions. As we clear out old ideas with different practices like Cord Cutting *(see page 122)*, we can work with the mind and body to repattern and rebuild. There is not one practice that will help you rewild; this entire book is designed to rewild you. The reclamation of self will naturally result in the rewilding and return to who you truly are, but it takes time. As a natural biproduct of you designing your practices around the things mentioned in this book, you will rewild yourself. In turn, you will unravel. You will reset. You will rebuild.

Gloria, the Roof Tree

Anna

Part of this book was inspired by the tree growing out of my friend's roof. Anna – a dream-weaving soul sister whose wisdom and creativity knows no-bounds – moved into a new apartment on Peace Street (Rua da Paz) just as I started writing this book. On Peace Street the birds sing louder than the passing cars. Just wait 'til you get inside. I call her place the fairy hideaway because it's exactly that. A giant mural of a magical garden hand-painted on the wall, disco ball planters hanging from the ceiling, Egyptian glass bottles filled with essential oils and homemade potions, freshly charged moon water, crystals, books, her vintage typewriter, and a bright red fireplace.

Obviously we're best friends.

One of the wildest things about this apartment is that there's literally a tree growing out of the roof. We named the tree Gloria – she's truly alive in all her glory. Even the birds stop by to celebrate her. Probably because one of them planted her! (We'll get to that in a moment).

The audacity of this tree to be growing out of the fucking roof is iconic. Go, Gloria, Go!

Gloria

How did she get there? It's safe to assume she was once a seed swallowed by a bird. That bird must've taken a big ol' shit on the roof and with a little water, a dream, and enough sunshine, BOOM. Gloria: A tree growin' out of the damn roof. If that isn't a metaphor for how shitty situations can turn into something beautiful then I don't know what is, babe. If you really think about it, generations of trees likely grow together in the same environment for decades. The apple doesn't fall far from the tree, remember?

Not this tree. Not Gloria. She left home. She was the Black Sheep in the family tree, and she's been through a lot of shit. Literally. Now she's up there rawdoggin' the rooftop, growing out of hot shingles. There's not even soil up there – it's insane! With a little grit, she had the audacity to root down in her own truth and she beat all odds. She bloomed beautifully. Not only does she have the best view in Lisbon, she made it all the way into this book. Next stop? Hollywood! I heard she's dating a tall palm planted outside of the Chateau Marmont, but who's to say? 'If they could see me now,' she screams from the rooftops of Lisboa. And see her now they can. If Gloria can turn shit into something beautiful, so can you, babe. So can you.

UPDATE: She's completely destroying the ceiling of the neighboring apartment, so she'll need to be removed. We're gonna replant her on my farm – again, with the big moves, Gloria! Lucky bitch... I mean birch. OK, let's move on. But let this tree be a message to all of us. We can rewild ourselves in any setting and Gloria has shown us how it's done. Tomorrow she may be gone, but for now she's up there pushing slightly sideways toward the sky.

Branch
out

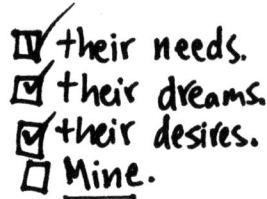
☑ their needs.
☑ their dreams.
☑ their desires.
☐ Mine.

Self-Sacrificing and People Pleasing

Stop saying yes when you want to say no.

Stop swallowing the words you want to speak.

Stop sacrificing your evening, your energy, or your truth, just to keep the peace.

How's that been working for you?

Right.

For many of us, the pattern of self-sacrificing was learned early. As kids, we had limited ways of understanding the world. When our needs weren't met, we told ourselves stories about why: *They don't care about me. My needs don't matter. To be loved, I must perform or betray myself.* Some of our deepest wounds were formed in the moments we chose safety over truth. We betrayed ourselves, and were rewarded. We did what we needed to do to keep the peace, the shelter, the support from our caretakers or communities. We all did this, to some degree. Self-betrayal shaped the way we see the world. We created narratives and belief systems around it. Overtime, these narratives get stronger as our ego searches for proof that supports them. The behavior becomes normalized as we grow up, and the patterns stick.

The mind is brilliant at creating patterns. It doesn't care if they're true or false, helpful or harmful, it just keeps running the program. And one of the most common programs is the people pleaser.

We all have an internal 'people pleaser.' My friend Anna once asked: What if your people pleaser doesn't need to disappear? What if you simply give it *a new job*?

Every single time you people-please, you sacrifice a piece of yourself for someone else.

Try this: Reassign your people pleaser to please you. Instead of scanning the room for what others need, ask yourself: *What do I need right now?*

It might be saying 'no' to the dinner you don't want to attend, and 'yes' to a quiet night in. It might be setting a boundary and letting someone be disappointed. It might be speaking up instead of holding back your comments to avoid rocking the boat. Small choices, but each one tells your system: *my needs matter too.*

This is permission to put yourself first. To reclaim the part of you that's always trying to keep the peace and redirect it inward. When you do, the 'peacekeeper' stops betraying you for others and becomes your ally.

What's *your* truth? What do *you* really want to do?

Great. Do that.

Change Your Environment, Not Yourself

When I began writing this book, I was in a new relationship. Letting someone that close triggers all kinds of shit. Almost weekly, I reminded myself to Pause with the panic *(see page 44)*, cry for a minute, or move any necessary energy. Sometimes I felt like I was walking the edge of a building. You know that feeling, like your stomach's gonna drop out your asshole? I knew he'd catch me if I ever fell flat on my ass, but still, when you get that rush of anxiety, and your stomach knots like you're gonna shit yourself, even a safety net can't keep you calm.

But what if that too is part of the experiment? Sitting there in the unknown. Panic. Let your stomach drop. Shit yourself. We're never gonna outrun it so we might as well sit with it and figure out what it's trying to tell you. This is one of those trigger moments where something is being flagged, something that needs to be looked at. *(Read about Shadow Work on page 87 and Triggers on page 71.)* It's another tool we can use to understand ourselves.

Part of me is terrified of speaking up and voicing my own needs. This shows up in all kinds of relationships. I'm afraid of being too much (back in elementary school I was always kicked out of class for being disruptive or bullied for being gay). But this is the work; being scared and doing it anyways. Are you nervous? Shaking? Cool. Do it while you shake. Just do it. Having the audacity to do the thing that scares the shit out of you, now that's real courage. Speak up for yourself. If you're in the right environment, the right people will hear you out. They'll accept you as you are. They'll accommodate, negotiate, and consider your needs (yes, these people really exist). I've experienced it. Over time I noticed that in this relationship it was safe for me to speak up, and he received it lovingly.

There's two important things to note: One, when you speak up and it's received by the right people it quite literally rewires your brain and recalibrates your nervous system into believing that *speaking up is safe*. This was the beautiful gift I received from this man. The second thing: If you speak up and someone does *not* receive it, then it's entirely your responsibility to accept their choice, and to place them in your life accordingly.

⌈Before you change yourself, try changing your environment.⌉

Trust people when they show you who they are. If they're inconsiderate, trust that. Some people *will* consider your feelings. If they wanted to, they would. Don't gaslight yourself or try to change people. Stop trying to force an asshole to be a pair of tiddies *(see People Are Trees on page 23)*. Witness others without judgment. Don't make their choices all about you. This isn't about you. This is about them in relation to you, and that's where your power lies. If he said I was way too much and he can't deal with it, then it's my job to leave. It's my job to place myself around considerate people who take my needs seriously. It's my job to creates boundaries for those who don't. If you're surrounded by people who think you're too much, then it's time for a little *Fuck This* energy *(see page 179)*. Fuck that.

Stop changing yourself to fit in your environment and change your environment to one that fits you.

Before I say anything, I like to witness *myself*. Similar to White Tantra, an ancient form of meditation, I simply witness, without reacting, whatever energy is moving through my body; emotionally, mentally, physically. This practice is extremely helpful at discharging our emotional response and neutralizing the stories we tell ourselves. Just feel and observe. Don't try to make sense of it or change it. Just feel it. Observe. It's that simple. We *can* feel without editing or adjustment. Breathe. Calm yourself down and witness what's moving with presence. Just the act of acknowledging our own panic, or joy, is already a step toward choosing how we respond. Journaling can take you even deeper. Ultimately, witnessing ourselves and noticing how we feel, emotionally, energetically, and physically, in relation to other people and environments is the number one way to understand where you should and shouldn't be.

Experiment with this. Notice how you feel in certain spaces and around certain people. Do you feel anxious? Are you second guessing yourself or feeling insecure? Do you feel disregarded or supported? Excited? Are you fueled for expansion and dreaming up what's possible? Every experience is a fork in the road; do you want to circle back and continue experiencing life with this person? Are your journeys aligned? Do you feel safe in this environment? Is there consideration, respect, and appreciation? If the answer is 'no', then, babe, it's time to go.

So, please, next time something feels off consider it might not be you that needs to change – it might be where you are. Choose a new place. Choose new people. And by all means, choose yourself.

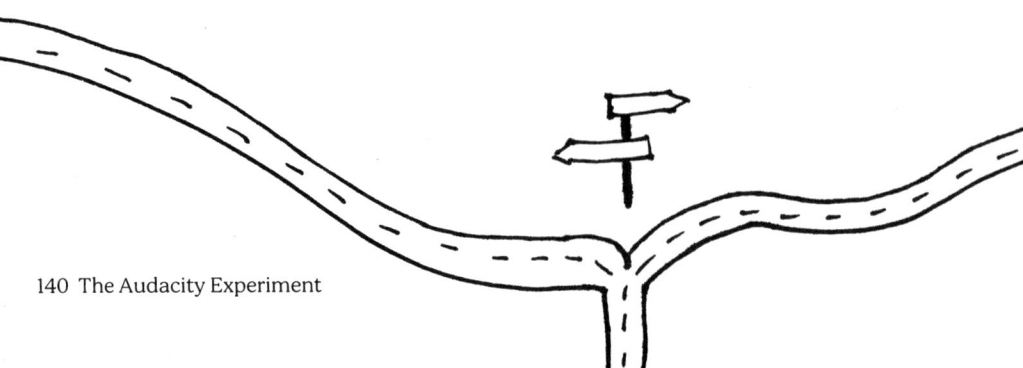

Where Are My People?

You know the saying, 'When the student is ready, the teacher appears'? Community is kinda like that, too. Authenticity attracts new people. The right people. Ones that match your vibe, literally. So don't be shocked when you start practicing these things and bitches start dropping like flies. Your energy field is adjusting. Things change. And so will the people you have around you. Not all of them, but a few for sure.

There are moments I've felt like, *Fuck, do I have any friends?* But three good friends are better than 30 shit-show soldiers. Quality, babe. Not quantity.

Better people *always* show up.

At first, it's a bit lonely. You can't really spread your wings and expect to feel seen by the ones who prefer the cage. You can't expect magic from someone with no abracadabra. There are moments where you feel like you can only talk about aliens, crystals, and chemtrails with the park bench prophet you just met feeding pigeons and casually predicting the fall of capitalism.

But, these are vine-swinging moments. Transient. You let go of one vine and haven't grabbed the next. You're airborne but you won't be floating forever. You'll land in a new timeline. And you'll meet great people, not just pigeon-feeding Pete.

There will be people you grow distant from. It can feel like a loss – I've lost friends, family, lovers. At times, it felt like I lost everything.

But how lucky we are to lose what we would not let go of ourselves.

As people exit our lives, they leave space for others to enter. So, get out there and meet them. Sign up for a Spanish class. Do yoga in the park. Learn to cook. Go bowling. Put yourself out there doing whatever it is that calls to you. It might feel awkward doing things alone at first. Go to dinner by yourself – I love to see movies alone. I can watch whatever I want and I don't need to share my popcorn. I don't fucking care what people think. Get comfortable with being uncomfortable. Dress how you want. Be yourself, without the need to assimilate. Drop the mask. Experience yourself without the performance. Authenticity attracts authenticity and soon you'll have a motley crew, a bunch of witches and weirdos like me and my friends. I have nine close friends now, babe – NINE! It's more than enough. One by one they showed up like the Universe had them standing in the curtains waiting for their cue. You'll find them when you get out there and starting unapologetically being you.

[
If you're alone now, be there. Alone is better than being poisoned by shitty people's influences. Take this time to meet yourself again. You'll meet others soon enough.
]

We all move through moments of decay and renewal. When you're authentic, everything inauthentic eventually dissolves. That's what creates space for new connections. The right community will gas you up and remind you that you're not crazy. All your big ideas, big feelings, and big moments – we're right there with ya. We'll help stretch your mind and see what's possible. Feeling safe here will repattern your nervous system, invite risk and reward, and remind you how it feels to be celebrated for all your wins, and held through your losses.

I want you to know we exist, and we're waiting for you.

You're not alone.

So, please, join us. This is your cue.

Find your people!

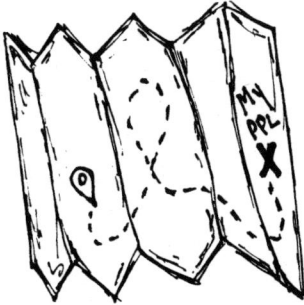

Relationships as Mirrors (The Four Fs)

The first thing I want to say about any relationship is that we might be asking too much of one person. You don't have to share every thought and emotion and latest obsession with one person in the hope that they can understand and relate to everything. Look around. Some people are great at giving advice. Some people are great at getting shitfaced. Sometimes those are not the same person.

My friend Anna and I grab bagels *and* give each other advice once a week in Lisbon; we call it Bagel Dia. I almost always walk in late and she's already eating a miso-chocolate chip cookie. She's an Aries with a sweet tooth so who am I to judge? Let people be who they are. If I wanted to be around a friend who doesn't have cookies before breakfast I would call someone else. But I like that she doesn't give a shit. Plus she gives great advice. And she shares her cookie.

Bagel Dia

Know your audience. Read the room. Not everyone can hold space for you like a trained therapist, and not everyone is supposed to. Feel into the connection, test the waters, and see how deep you can dive with the person. If you find yourself in the shallow end, find another pool. Or keep things light – not every connection needs to take you to the depths of your soul. That being said, sometimes we need depth, or support, or advice. Have you ever tried diving into the shallow end? I fucking hope not. That's why they paint 'NO DIVING' all over the shallow end of the pool – because you'll get seriously injured if you try to dive there. People are not the same, and some people are no-diving-shallow-end-of-the-pool kinda people, and that's okay. They might not have the capacity to hold you in that space. We can't expect a dentist to save us from a burning building, and we wouldn't go to the zoo for a root canal, would we? Some people are good for tacos but not for trauma. Let them be who they are and place them accordingly.

As you move through your day, each person that you interact with is teaching you something about yourself. Each person is mirroring something back to you. These mirrors invite a deeper understanding of your own psyche. Some moments might trigger the shit out of you – great, that's likely flagging a pain point you can look at to better understand yourself. *(See Triggers and Flags on page 71.)* But these mirrors aren't just reflecting back to us what we need to work through, they also reflect back a world of possibility. As you read my writing, I'm mirroring the possibility and potential of you becoming a writer. Moments of laughter with friends are reflecting available joy and connection. The happy couple in the park is revealing the possibility of love. The other couple in the park screaming at each other is reflecting back to you the possibility of somethin' else. You get the point. If you're looking at life through the lens of learning you'll find something in everything.

We can work with this data to understand where to place people in our lives accordingly. If your mom is incapable of having a conversation with you that lands at the same depth as a therapist, then maybe you need a therapist and not your mother to trauma dump on. Someone who's trained and qualified to support you. We've all had that one party friend who's here today, gone tomorrow. Don't expect them to help you pick up the pieces when your life falls apart and you need some anchored stability. Maybe you need a martini and a meltdown, and they're perfect for that!

Choose wisely.

Maybe you need a 7:00 a.m. U-Haul pick up for your cross-country move, and they're not your person. Manage your expectations. Understand who people are, and adjust yourself accordingly.

People often assign a role or task to someone they unconsciously know can't meet their needs so they can reinforce the subliminal narrative and continue looping through the idea that no one can meet their needs. This is often rooted in our needs not being met as a child, so we continue to play out this dynamic in hopes of a different outcome. The outcome only changes when we believe we deserve to have our needs met, we truly understand where people are at in relationship to our needs, and we align ourselves with the proper individuals to ensure our needs are met. Sometimes nibbling nachos is all we need, other times it's a nervous breakdown, but rarely are those two things with the same person. If you're lucky enough to find yourself an Aries like Anna you can have it all (these people are rare, but they do exist!).

I've found that the deepest reflections and strongest mirrors for me are people that fall into a few specific categories, which I call The Four Fs. These people create the most intense experiences across the board and help us understand ourselves on a psychological, emotional, and energetic level. Here are the categories. Drumroll please...

The Four Fs

1. Friends

2. Family

3. Finances

4. And the people you Fuck

Begin to witness what parts of you are most active when you're in any kind of relationship, but especially with someone who falls into any of the Four Fs.

I've found we really attract three types of people into our life: some people are like Non-Playable Characters in a video game; they're background actors floating through the world with us, passing us on the street but we don't have much of a direct connection with them. The second are the people who reflect back to us possibility. They show us what is possible for us, both good and bad, and sometimes show us how far we've come, what we want to avoid, or where we might want to go next. The last group of people are our high-impact teachers – these are the people who largely fall into the Four Fs. We connect with them directly and likely often, we're in intimate spaces with them (not just sexually intimate), and they often mirror back to us our deepest wounds and highest potential. These people often have the same emotional dynamics and patterning, energetic vibrations, and psychological wounds as us. Or, they possess the power to heal and adjust those wounds. They can present as prey vs. predator, a trauma bond, Codependent dynamics, The Drama Triangle *(see page 114)*. These connections can also be rooted in joy, support, expansion, creation and play.

I've noticed that most relationships are either maintaining energetic harmony with one another, supporting growth and expansion, or helping acknowledge deep wounds that keep us from accessing our own true power (and potentially helping heal those same wounds as well). Like when two eagles are mating and they fly at each other then spiral down toward the Earth (that's insane), we enter a spiralic journey with one another where we either heal together, expand and experience the highest potential expression of our relationship, or we leave people where they're at when we've grown beyond them. The Four Fs help bridge the gap between who you are and who you have the potential to be.

Let's imagine a scenario where you're meeting with a potential new client. This relationship would go under Finances. Maybe y'all decide to meet at Wheelhouse – this amazing social wellness hub for conscious creators. It's an insanely beautiful space, I know the owner (it's me – the guy who wrote this book). The imported Japanese matcha is to die for. Let's pretend you're all matcha'd up and buzzing green with excitement about the prospect of this new project. The conversation takes a turn toward money and next thing you know you're breaking a sweat. The client, let's call her Portia, mentions her budget for this project is only $750. Your thoughts: *I was thinking more like $2,500 for the amount of work I know this is going to take.* But you find yourself unable to speak up.

Come visit

This is a good example of one of the ways mirroring works. Now you're presented with two options.

1. Option One

Notice what pain point is triggered and what energy is active within you. Maybe you're feeling undervalued and nervous about communicating your worth and your needs. That's the shallow-end experience. It's important to recognize the 'here and now' energy and then, depending on where you are, maybe pin it for a deep dive later on to truly understand where it stems from, and work through shifting it if need be. For now, gently wrap up the conversation and let Portia know she's a cheap bitch. I'm kidding. Let her know you'll have to review the workload and follow up with an email if you find yourself having a panic attack in the middle of Lisbon's most beautiful café. Or, if at all possible, speak up for yourself now and create a solid boundary around your price and her budget.

2. Option Two

A deep dive. Wrap up the conversation as quickly as possible and while your heart is still pounding in your asshole go and sit with yourself somewhere quiet. Observe your emotional response and what is moving through you. A sense of disrespect? Scarcity around not having enough money? Maybe a feeling that you're not being heard, again. A dive into the deep end of this experience would look like reviewing other times in your life when you felt this way. There was an experience, probably at a younger age, where you likely felt this exact emotion. When was that? What was happening and what story or belief was built around that experience and how does that affect you and the way you see the world around you now? Remember, that emotion is tied to a feeling. That feeling creates a story, and that story creates a belief. This is how emotional patterning is developed.

Here's a quick example:

Triggered Emotion →

Feeling Neglected ↓

"They don't care about me" (the story) ↓

"My needs don't matter" (the belief)

The Universe, and your mind that's helping create your experience of the Universe, is not considering what's 'good' or 'bad' for you. It's just giving you what you are, and what you 'are' stems from your beliefs about yourself and what you deserve, and how you feel, and the actions you take based on those feelings. This is the mirror. Well, it's part of it. The mirror helps show us where we're at, what's working, and what we might need to sort out. The Universe will keep bringing you more and more people and situations that reflect these stories back to you, in the hope that you can recognize the pattern and break it. The challenges are helping us find solutions. Real solutions. Solutions that will recalibrate our beliefs and our energy field. Okay, but how do we shift it? In this case, by getting rid of the belief, 'My needs don't matter.'

Yes, they do. Your needs matter. Say this out loud: *'My needs matter.'* If you didn't say it, go back and SAY IT! If you're in public, whisper it under your breath for all I care but say it. 'MY NEEDS FUCKING MATTER!!'

Shifting these things takes time, and patience, and love, and patience, and compassion, and more patience, but they *will* shift overtime! I've done it. And now my needs matter most (well, I'm almost there, but they matter more than they used to!).

This is why working with the moon cycles is so powerful. A New Moon in any sign becomes a Full Moon in that same sign six months later. That means we can work with those energies for 180 days and literally shift our experience. Commit to one six-month cycle and see what happens – set intentions under the New Moon, take aligned action as the moon waxes, release and let go at the Full Moon, and integrate as it wanes. I literally guide thousands and thousands of people worldwide through these New Moon and Full Moon practices every two weeks online. It's a recorded 25-minute video and you can pay-what-you-want to watch it. No excuses, babe. Watch the fucking workshop and change your life. You can also align your shadow work with these six-month cycles. Whatever it is that you're clearing, or weaving, these Moon cycles will amplify the energy and help manifest it sooner. Okay, now back to penny-pinching Portia and your sweaty brow.

At this point you probably have a pit in your stomach; maybe you're even red in the face with frustration and resentment. Great. Noticing what's happening in your body is super helpful. How are your emotions? That energy-in-motion is pumping through your body, no doubt – how does it feel? *(see Your Body Is Technology on page 35 and Emotions: What*

Are They? on page 52). Okay, so you're feeling triggered to some degree, and for good reason, and now you're presented with those two options we mentioned above. Let's say you go with Option One because you don't have time for a full deep dive right now. Let's say you're also feeling your most audacious self and you DGAF what people think about you, so you decide to speak up, flex your boundaries, and gently push back to explore what it feels like standing in your power and acknowledging your worth.

'Unfortunately, that budget won't work for me with the current scope of work,' you respond confidently, fairly certain you just shit yourself. Portia maybe says:

'Oh... okay.'

The knot in your stomach tightens.

'I'll have to circle back after chatting with my team but if you send over a proposal, I could likely meet your standard rate.'

And BOOM. You just planted a seed that will bloom into the most confident, self-advocating, expansive version of you yet. Why? Because you've recalibrated your energy field into deeper alignment with voicing your opinion. You're repatterning your brain into self-preservation instead of performance for acceptance. Your nervous system is beginning to understand there's no real threat in asking for what you need. Like all seeds, it's your responsibility to nurture, water, and protect it so it grows. But, babe, you planted that shit. You did well.

Let's do one more example, something that hits a bit closer to home for me and my daddy issues. Maybe you're in a relationship with someone and they say they're going out for dinner, but the details are vague. You expect them home by 10:00 and by 10:30 you start texting, but you get no answer. The phone goes straight to voicemail.

Sound the alarms and grab a bucket cuz I'm seriously about the throw up.

I've had more than a few relationships where my partners treated truth and loyalty quite casually and honesty felt negotiable. I have other childhood shit rooted in a similar energy, and it wired my nervous system baseline into hypervigilance around this sort of thing. Your person isn't necessarily cheating or lying about where they're at, but it's possible you've slipped into panic mode based on a past pattern and your nervous system can't differentiate between a real and perceived threat.

Maybe something makes you feel like you can't trust the person in your life right now, but it's something that happened in the past with a different person. If you were at an audition, you'd be reading from the wrong script. We might bring old baggage into new relationships, but we need to feel safe enough with our new partners to talk things through. This is the only way to reprogram our nervous systems and rewrite a new relational story. You can't do that on your own, unfortunately. Part of it, yes, but some things can only be healed in true partnership.

We need to see people for who they are and not through our lens of the worst possible outcome. We can use tools such as nonviolent communication to share our needs in any given situation. I read a book by Marshall Rosenberg on nonviolent communication that really helped me reshape things; basically, it helped me talk about what I saw instead of what I'm feeling – for example, 'You interrupted me' vs. 'You're rude!' It helped me learn how to share feelings, and not blame, and to ask for what I need clearly, instead of passively aggressively or straight-up aggressively (it's that Italian blood I've got in me!). It helped me better understand my needs and directly ask for what I need, but the other important part of this is making sure I ask the right person. 'Portia, I'm looking at your current budget and it feels out of alignment with the workload,' is a safer, gentler way to nudge her toward meeting your needs as a service provider. That'll likely keep the conversation flowing better than saying, 'Portia, you

Great Book! [handwritten annotation with arrow pointing to "by Marshall Rosenberg"]

broke bitch, I hate this conversation and your low-ass budget is insulting me.' If you lovingly share your opinion, and that person isn't able to meet your needs, then it's up to you to choose if you're okay with that. If not, then negotiate something that still feels good, or ask someone else. Don't project your anger, or pain from the past, onto them. It's unlikely they are the real root of that pain, and it's not fair we judge people for not being who we think they should be, or for not acting how we think they should act.

If you find yourself triggered and likely reacting to an old wound instead of the situation in front of you, here's a cheat sheet to get you through the immediate moment, or to support the deep dive:

Cheat Sheet

Immediate Support:

- Breath work *(see page 41)*

- 5-4-3-2-1 Grounding Technique *(see page 42)*

- White Tantra (non-judgmental witnessing of emotions; *see page 140)*

Deeper Supportive Techniques:

- Journaling *(see page 89)*

- Shadow Work *(see page 87)*

- Cutting Cords *(see page 122)*

Think of an example where you start looking at a situation through a lens of fear and anxiety based on something that happened in the past. This is the beauty and struggle of Mercury, the planet that rules our mind. In Greek mythology Mercury is depicted as Hermes, the messenger God who can time travel and visit both heaven and the underworld, bringing back messages to Earth. Like Mercury, our mind doesn't obey rules of space and time. Our mind can quickly move between timeframes and perceived realities, both literally and metaphorically dancing through the realms of possibility. Modern neuroscience shows that humans are the only species with 'episodic foresight' and honestly sometimes that shit works against us. This means we have the ability to quite literally rummage through the past reconstructing our worst fears and experiencing them as if they're happening now, or to build out a vivid idea of the future and feel it as both expansive or contractive depending on the storyline we're building. Maybe we're conjuring up exciting opportunities. Maybe we're imagining worst-case scenarios.

Mercury also rules our nervous system. So think about the mind–body connection and how thoughts, good or bad, true or not, are setting the tone for our nervous system. Adequate or inadequate nervous system regulation triggers our emotions, which influences our choice of words and actions. Now imagine all of that being dysregulated because of unprocessed experiences from the past or consistent fear-based thinking about the future. Imagine that running your life, unconsciously. It's not a cute look.

Let's circle back to this example of your lying, cheating partner who's currently out fucking your best friend behind your back, while saying they're at dinner with friends. Or maybe that's just the story in your head, even if it's super unlikely to be true. I joke (only because I've been there), but let's say you texted, you called, and they still don't respond. Now what?

Where does your mind go?

How does your body feel?

What story shows up?

maybe you

Maybe for some of you, it's nothing. You're totally cool – that's a good sign. It means you're regulated because you've done the work (good job) or maybe you've never experienced that kind of betrayal in the past (you lucky duck!).

If you're like me, and you've gone through the betrayals, then maybe you're still dealing with some of the shadows and you might want to turn to page 87. That section will bring you through supportive shadow work to help you release and integrate these energies. Maybe you're good and looking to enhance more of the light side. Then turn to Arts and Creativity on page 242. This section helps us understand why creative expression is a vital part of our expansive nature.

Since every person we meet and every experience we have can mirror something back to us, there's no possible way to examine every mirror. You'll go crazy and I don't suggest turning your life into an opportunity to 'notice and fix everything about yourself.' I've been stuck in that loop before and constantly thinking about the ways in which we're defective doesn't leave much space for joy or play. You're not here to problem solve all day long. You're here to live your life.

I mentioned earlier these mirrors reflect beauty, peace, love, joy, excitement, and all that good stuff as well. We can experience a mirroring of love, of peace, and of bliss and all kinds of positive emotions. We're often faster to grasp onto negatives than positives, so watch for that. A lot of this is patterning and conditioning. We're wired to keep ourselves safe and stay on guard for what's wrong or what could go wrong. We're conditioned to be in competition with each other, fighting over the same capitalist dream or whatever they're selling us. We've learned to carry shame and guilt and fear (ideologies from certain religions, family, and societal norms) so that we feel disempowered. We then seek answers, validation, and approval outside of ourselves. I talk about shame and fear and guilt often because, for a lot of us, it keeps rearing its ugly ass head back up. If you knew your true power (you're the Mother of Dragons, remember? *See page 85*), if you presented yourself without shame, if you moved through the world without guilt and fear, you would be unstoppable. You *are* unstoppable. It's this bullshit that keeps you thinking you're not.

We can get so stuck on one side of the story, like how shitty that person made us feel or whatever, and we'll use that to reinforce a story of some kind, something like *I feel so disconnected from the world and I hate all these people* (I've been there). These hidden aspects of our psyche often overlook all the beauty and all the ways we're made to feel good. They will deny a bid for connection or reject invitations for intimacy and friendship or community, because we're so jaded from the past, or because we still carry stories of unworthiness or separation. We'll unconsciously create more issues and separation in our life just to complain about it and reinforce the storylines. If we do this long enough, the stories become calcified in our energy field and it then becomes a personality trait.

We all know that one person who is always moping around, or the one who can't get over what happened to them 12 years ago, or the hyper-independent friend who DOESN'T NEED NO MAN because all men suck! So on and so forth. They've been consumed by the story. They're too attached to their lens. Alternative lenses = alternative realities (*see People and Projections on page 159*). We don't have to focus on the 'shit in the mirror' but rather we can start finding all the beauty staring back at us. If we've seen life as ugly, unfair, and unsatisfying for years and years then we definitely need more time to chisel away the calcification of these old stories, but we *can* shift the stories and start viewing life through a new lens. I've chipped away at some stories for years, and I'm experiencing life on the other side of it. It takes time, but you'll get there.

We're here to play, to experiment, to pick a path and change direction. We're here to see what works, what's beautifully expansive, what feels good, and to realize, *Wait, this is not where I want to go!* and shift again. So change direction. Or go back! Take a diagonal path. Do a fucking cartwheel and cut through a meadow full of wildflowers that you never even noticed. Stop. Smell the roses. Enjoy yourself a little.

Smell me.

When you intentionally create more space for joy to be reflected back to you, you'll begin to find yourself surrounded by people who believe in your process, your gifts, and your mission. You'll experience a deeper connection with yourself, with nature and with people. Sometimes that deeper connection can only be experienced after you've moved through a pain point together. Have you heard anyone describe intimacy as 'into-me-see'? This kind of intimacy stems from us being honest with ourselves about what we're truly feeling, whether experiencing love or pain, friction or flow. When we have a pain point triggered, it's our responsibility to acknowledge it first, then figure out how to communicate that effectively to those around us. Sharing those parts of ourselves with others takes vulnerability. We're letting them see into us. If they can meet us in that space, accept who we are, and make adjustments, while we both compromise to see what works for the connection, the result is a beautiful expansion into true intimacy, providing the closeness we all seek.

Closeness is about presence, not proximity.

As humans we all strive for real connection, and that's only achieved through presence, truth, and respect. We may not necessarily feel deeply connected or emotionally close to some of the people we spend most of our time with. We might feel there's some depth, in some ways, but not to the degree required for true safety and love. It's about being seen for who you are, being safe enough to express that, and being around healthy people willing to compromise with you and provide a middle ground where you can both meet each other. You must extend that back to them as well. Only through presence can we develop real intimacy and close connection. Connection doesn't always come with closeness, just like proximity doesn't always come with presence.

People and Projections

We see all people, the world, and the situations around us through our own filters, not as they *actually* are. Sometimes we see closer to the truth of 'who' someone is or 'what' something means, but there are always three truths: yours, theirs, and the ultimate unseen truth.

Simultaneously Layered

1. **Your Truth** is completely shaped by your experience of the past, your biases, emotions, culture, family, traumas, limitations, and fears... everything that has been metabolized and integrated, and everything that's still unprocessed. All these influences contribute to creating your truth.

2. **Their Truth** is built from all the same things as your truth, but shaped through their eyes and experiences. Their truth reflects all their processed and unprocessed mental clutter – their conditioning, experiences, and emotional state. What someone else thinks is possible for you is what they think is possible for them. Where other people limit themselves, they limit you, perhaps unconsciously so.

3. **The Ultimate Unseen Truth** is the reality that exists beyond everyone's perception. It's pure, neutral, and void of any emotional charge or triggering power. It's truth on the deepest layer, where only God, the Universe, or our Creator can see what's really going on.

We can only get closer to the ultimate unseen truth through humility, conversation, and deep awareness, but we'll never fully grasp it through our limited human capacity. That's not really the point anyway. We're *supposed* to trigger each other with various versions of the truth; that friction allows us to reshape and reformat ourselves into the highest possible expression *(see Triggers and Flags on page 71)*. It helps us find harmony in our relationships. We can trigger joy, we can trigger anger, but each trigger acts like waves crashing into stone. Over time we shape a coastline, a collage of edges, both smooth and sharp, a constellation of our contributions to one another with each meeting point carving out a larger landscape of our collective identity. We are a living shoreline shaped by every sunrise and every storm we've survived.

> Keep this in mind whenever you're engaging with someone – they can only see you as expansively as they see themselves. They can only meet you as deeply as they have met themselves. If they see something as impossible for you, it's only that they see it as impossible for themselves.

We must surround ourselves with people who gas us up; people who believe we can, because they believe *they* can, or at least they think that someone, somewhere is audacious enough to make it possible. Remember, most reactions are not about you. It's like when you're not invited out with the 'cool kids' and you convince yourself it's because you're a fucking loser... then later you realize you're never invited because you don't do cocaine. You're not missing out, you're riding a different wave, but you made up a story about how lame you are. Keep riding your own wave (especially if that wave isn't a fat line of coke. No judgment, that's just not a loop I'm looking to get caught in again – but we'll talk about that another time.)

 Our separate truths can leave us in completely different realities, and they do. Most people's reactions are about what has happened in their past, not about the present, and it's not about you. Arguments are often just layers of projection crashing into each other, not actual facts colliding. Look at the ongoing conversations around Indigenous sovereignty, global movements for safety, human rights, and self-determination. These situations show us that multiple truths can coexist at the same time – communities seeking protection, land, identity, and dignity, all at once, none of it simple, and none of it one-sided. Coexistence is the goal, not competing wounds or competing truths. We don't have to collapse into projection. We can choose compassion, complexity, and a wider lens.

In any given day, we see multiple projections colliding as the world unravels and unfolds. I know sometimes it feels like a downward spiral, but I promise the intensity is supposed to crack us open to deeper understanding, compassion, and adjustments that will eventually lead to a beautiful outcome. Sometimes the drama needs to get really loud before we pay attention. Projections create distortion and emotional noise that blocks our ability to hear or connect with each other. Alternatively, our awareness of these projections helps break the cycles and manage ourselves accordingly. Awareness is really the only way out.

✱ Remember, all experiences are neutral until we attach meaning to them. There's an unconscious filtering system in our psyche that automatically decides what it means and then our feelings, triggered by our emotions, typically encourage a reaction. When we're aware of this process it's easier for us to interrupt it. It's no longer an automatic circuit; we can experience something, intentionally create meaning, and choose how we wish to respond. This is what liberates us. This is how we realign with a new timeline. This is how we drift (*read about drifting on page 17*).

So experiment. Try to zoom out and see what's *really* happening when different versions of the truth seem to be clashing. Yours, others, mine. Where is there friction and where is there flow? What resonates with you and what doesn't?

And stop taking people's projections so seriously; don't live in their reality. Create your own.

Why the Fuck Are You Talking?

I often ask myself this question, and quietly, in my mind, ask other people the same thing. Especially if they're talking at me instead of to me. I don't mean to be rude, but I'm really asking, *What part of the psyche is talking right now, and why?*

[Which part of ourselves is driving this conversation?]

Every voice we speak from has an agenda. This is true for you, me, and everyone in between. These voices are rooted in something, somewhere, trying to know something, or get somewhere. Our conversations can be rooted in love, fear, ego, curiosity, anything! But each of these voices has its own desired outcome – in other words, there's a reason you're asking that question or saying that thing. The words we use shape our reality *(see The Vibration of Vocabulary on page 205)*, but on an even deeper level, they can also reveal it. If you begin to pay attention to yourself and others, you'll be able to read between the lines. You'll begin to hear what's unspoken. You may find through their tone, posture, and emotional charge that there is more going on beneath the surface. Something you can sense, something you can feel. Something unsaid.

Now, don't go crazy and get lost overanalyzing every conversation you have, because you'll literally go mad – but I do think that there are times where we need to understand what's really being said and what's really going on. (This can sometimes come in handy in communications with your Four Fs; *see page 144.*) Use this powerful tool on yourself to begin to understand what your conversations are revealing about yourself. The 'part' of you that's speaking might not even be your true self, or it might not be reflective of where you are in this present moment, or what you really want.

- Are you talking from a wounded place?

- Are your questions rooted in fear or scarcity?

- Is this a projection of a parent's voice or idea?

- Is it an unconscious part of yourself that holds a lot of anger? (If it's the part that holds anger, ask yourself what's underneath it. Anger is a secondary emotion.)

When we're aware of the different parts of ourselves that can be activated it's easier to spot patterns. Is part of you screaming to be heard? What exhausted part of you needs a little love? Are you *really* angry that they forgot to put extra ketchup in your takeout bag, or are you deeply frustrated because you feel like no one ever fucking listens to you? Maybe that's where the anger actually stems from and your psyche is just looking for an outlet to release all the backed-up energy. Maybe you just want to be heard and it has nothing to do with ketchup.

These voices can create unnecessary conflict; if your wounded self is trying to chat with someone else's toxic ego self then expect all hell to break loose. But if you identify your speaker you can manage yourself in a better way. Identifying the other person's speaker helps too – just keep it to yourself. Almost nobody responds well to hearing, 'I think your ego is talking right now.'

If you're lucky enough to be around another person who can also self-monitor, true connection can happen on a whole new level. Both people can remain honest and in integrity. You'll be able to monitor what part of you is most alive and you can put it into practice by saying things like, 'There's a part of me that feels crazy because you came home late and I have all these stories swirling in my head about where you were and who you were with and I fucking hate this feeling.' And from my experience, a healthy person should be able to respond with something like, 'Oh shit, I hate that for you. I just got caught up at dinner because I ran into an old friend and we had a second coffee so things ran late, but all is good. Next time I'll text you or something if that helps.' This exists, by the way. Someone who you can share all parts of yourself with, and even better, if you can identify who or what part is speaking, they can help you re-regulate that part. I say this because I actually had this in my last relationship and it was wild – it repatterned my nervous system like never before, and it allowed me to create real intimacy and a sense of peace and calm. For the first time I felt truly safe in sharing what I needed to share. I was heard. I was fully accepted. And that also made the sex amazing. Well, the sex isn't overly relevant here but it had the quiet authority of something that mattered, and it's the kind of detail that changes the flavor of the story, so there we have it. Anyways, find someone you can explore all your voices with. Find someone who can accept all the voices that are dying to be heard, and find someone who can help you reconcile the anxious ones. Find someone you love, someone who loves you, and someone you love to fuck. They exist.

I promise!

Cringe

This is your permission slip to be cringe. We started the book off with a permission slip so you remember every day that you can and should do whatever the fuck you want (as long as you're safe and not hurting anyone). Sometimes that means posting that TikTok, or signing up for adult Musical Theatre camp, being the oldest person in the classroom, or randomly buying a violin and learning to play like I just did. I want you to embrace the cringe. I want you to experiment with *Oh My God, am I actually gonna post/do/say this!?* Yes. Why? Because your cringe could be your golden ticket.

After riding the struggle bus for some time, about ten years after I graduated as an American Sign Language English Interpreter, I landed a six-figure contract and thought I had it all figured out. Fast-forward 90 days and I was flat on my face again with nothing but minimal savings, having been pushed out of a community to which I'd seemingly given my entire life. (A story for another time.) It was an emotional, financial, and mental rock bottom and I was not okay.

Thankfully I'd met my mentor years earlier and had been learning tarot, reiki, and other spiritual stuff. I started taking one-on-one clients and built a decent list of regulars. I was charging pennies because I had imposter syndrome and couldn't believe this work had serious value to it. (In hindsight, that makes me cringe, and not in a good way.) But still, I was making okay money. I remember watching tarot readers on YouTube and I thought, why not post my own? In the first two hours I had like 87 views and three comments. People were connecting with my reading. YouTube was easy for me. Chill. No cringe detected.

Loser!

About two months later I thought, *Why not post this on Instagram? Wait, but Instagram is cool... everyone's on there being models, and photographers, and I'm gonna start doing tarot? Who the fuck do I think I am? Ew. Cringe.* At that time, no one was doing tarot or anything really like that on IG, at least from what I was seeing/following. So I didn't either. Until one day, I did. I remember the first time I ever posted it was a two-and-a half-hour long tarot reading with all 12 zodiac signs in one clumsy video of me sweating my ass off, hiccupping and stumbling on my words. I was a fucking train wreck.

I'm such a loser, I thought to myself during the livestream in moments when my intuition felt like it was shutting down. Stage fright. Everyone's watching. *WTF are they thinking about me? Ew, I hate this, but I'm already at Capricorn, just FOUR more horoscopes, keep going or it'll be worse, you didn't even finish!? What a LOSER! Fuck me.*

I continued to trip over my words like Bambi learning to walk. I felt so fucking cringe! Now looking back I realize cringe is just in my emotional scar tissue. It's triggering a wound connected to another time I expressed myself and someone made fun of me. We don't fear being ourselves, we fear being unwelcome as we are. And courage and expression are the antidote to cringe. We need to stop giving a fuck what people think. Trust me, it works. We need to work with the cringe to repattern the reaction. Cringe really only exists when we're waiting for approval, or permission. Sometimes we might put ourselves out there, cringe, and still feel like we failed. Don't stop working your cringe muscle. Put yourself out there again, in all your glory, because that cringe could eventually be a catalyst for something big. Now if I do an IG Live some people hang on my every word – I feel so empowered and aligned with my soul and service. Back then? I was living a livestreamed nightmare. We did once unknowingly livestream a mental breakdown I had (but we'll save that story for another day – maybe you saw it live? Please like and subscribe!).

After I snapped back into my body, I smoked a fat bowl of engineered Canadian weed, that intense biohacking white man kinda weed that could render a moose unconscious, ordered a pizza, and passed the fuck out. I think I was in some type of trauma response from the unplanned shock therapy of that sweaty IG Live. Yet the book you're holding in your hands is the fruit from the branch of the tree that grew from that seed I unknowingly planted that day.

The audacity to put myself out there. Terrifying (yet eventually very fruitful). Herein lies the invitation: Where can you activate your cringe? Experiment with it. If you feel weird, or awkward, or sweaty maybe it's because you're at the edge of your comfort zone, and maybe that's where your million-dollar idea or book deal, is waiting for you. It was waiting for me. So, to cringe or not to cringe? That is the question. I say go for it, Bambi. Cringe away.

Protecting Your Energy

The Earth has provided many beautifully supportive elements to help us protect our peace; we just need to know where to look and how to use them. Working with crystals and herbs, connecting intentionally with nature and the elements, and using oils, sigils, and symbols can all contribute to protecting, clearing, or enhancing our energy field.

We all have an auric field, our aura. This is an energetic field that surrounds our body – it presents itself in layers and colors, it takes on certain shapes and curves, and it can help you understand the current state of the physical, emotional, mental, and spiritual body by observing it. It also acts as an antenna that picks up the energies in a space around you. To perceive the aura is to see it, sense it, or feel it. My mentor once told me that our auras can expand up to 30 feet!

Our auras help us understand our environments, but they can also pick up stray energies in the same way our body can catch a flu or cold. Do you ever randomly feel sadness, anxiety, or fear? It might be coming from a friend, family member, a lover, or even their collective energies. We can pick up ideas, entities (don't be scared by this term), attachments, stories, projections, or fears in the space around us and proceed to carry them along thinking they are our own. They're not. These energetic cords or attachments can blur the lines between what's ours and what isn't. This is why we need to protect and clean our own energy.

I love my mom, but she can be a bit of a worry wart (and for good reason!). I remember when the pandemic was first unfolding and I was trying to decide if I should fly back to Canada or stay in Portugal. The Universe was really taking care of me at that time. I was dating a cute, caring, supportive guy who had an amazing network. I had access to food, medicine, housing, and everything I needed. My online tarot and astrology was really starting to grow and I had cash coming in. I was fine.

Mom wasn't.

The Canadian government, my friends, and most of my family were on mom's side – 'CHRISTOPHER! COME HOME!' was the message I got on repeat. I knew she was serious because she called me Christopher but it still didn't feel right to leave. Everyone else's thoughts, ideas, fears, and projections were floating in my energy field. I was constantly cleaning and clearing things out, but every couple of days... BOOM. 'CHRISTOPHER!' and the voices were back. This is why it's so important for us to clean our energy regularly (see page 117).

It's not just your personal energy that needs protection, it's also your space, and you should clean the energy on a regular basis, preferably every day, with an intentional ritual. (Don't be scared of the word ritual; go to page 232.) I also think it's a good idea to work with other people once a month to get a real deep clean since we all have blind spots. I love to use salt for cleansing and protection – I'll take a bath with it or scrub in the shower, sometimes I'll mix water and sea salt and sprinkle it around my house. I also use crystals, visuals, and symbols I've learned along the way. I wear talismans (jewelry designed or purchased with a specific intention) to keep my energy clean and protected, and even then, things sometimes slip through the cracks.

When we protect our energy, we preserve it. If we're constantly thinking or worrying about stuff that feels like ours but isn't, that becomes a major energetic leak. Your field is a sacred space, and the more you share it the more depleted you can become, as your own energy get lost in the mix. Energetic protection doesn't shut down your intuition or vitality. It helps filter out what's not yours and allows you to be intentional and deliberate when it comes to the energy you allow into your space. Welcome to boundaries, babe.

let's Explore!

Boundaries
are your Best Friend.

Anchoring Your Energy

We are exposed to more information in a single day than our ancestors were in a lifetime and our nervous systems, our brains, were not designed for that. Every day we're slammed from all angles: social media, news, work, conversations, podcasts, and whatever other bullshit is thrown our way. We're casually scrolling past images of horror from Gaza, Sudan, Syria, Ukraine, or whatever region is burning this week. Never has there been so much money accumulated and this many kids going hungry. Our brains cannot process that amount of suffering. And that's just the external world — some of us can't even keep the voices in our head quiet long enough to take a shit in peace.

This level of turbulence isn't normal — but we do what we can to manage it.

If we're not careful, our energy can get distorted by all this and more. It also happens in crowds, and relationships. Maybe you're picking up stress from someone standing beside you. You might feel sad or randomly think about an ex you dumped a while back (even though they're a fart funnel and you're completely over it). Maybe you're feeling anxious but really it's your mom's energy because she called you twice, your phone was on silent, and now she thinks you're tied up in someone's basement (why do they always jump to worst-case scenarios?). Either way, their energy has found its way to you. And you need to clean it up. It's kinda like stepping in dog shit; you need to wash it off your shoe. *(If this is resonating check out the Cord Cutting on page 122 as well as the section on Boundaries on page 175.)*

Now imagine all the noise from the energetic projections and distortions that come from movies, music, religion, government, mass media, your family's unhealed generational trauma, other people's fears and limiting beliefs – I could go on. If you're not taking steps to protect your energy, you're vulnerable to what I call psychic attacks or energetic distortions from the rest of the world.

✳ Remember: *your* frequency sets the tone for your reality. If you're lost in the influence of other people's emotions, energies, and realities, you're not creating your own. You'll get pulled into their stress, their drama, their bullshit. Anchoring your energy allows you to choose. It means you create more consciously because it settles you back into your own desired state of being. This practice is especially important when we're moving through transition, illness, discomfort, distress, or chaos of any kind. When the ship gets rocked in the waves of chaos, that's when it's most critical to anchor back into ourselves.

Okay great, well how TF do we actually do that? Take these three simple steps:

1. Notice the noise

2. Center yourself

3. Shift your state

remember this!

I said it's simple, not easy. Here's how we do it:

Notice the Noise

Our own shadows and fears contribute to the mess, and often when we're experiencing someone else's energy, it presents as our own. You feel your mom's anxiety, but it won't show up the same way. You feel panic, the same vibration, but with a different storyline. You translate it into your own. Energy is contagious, but it shapeshifts. Your mom thinks you've been kidnapped, and you think your stomach pain is a death sentence. These are the moments we anchor. We anchor back into what is our own. We anchor into what we want to feel. We anchor to turn down the volume of everything and everyone else. But we can only anchor into silence after we notice the noise. Don't bypass the discomfort – do the opposite. Take ten minutes to have a little human meltdown. Then remember you're a creative, spiritual, energetic being and work with the technology of your beautiful body. Center yourself, and shift your state.

Center Yourself

Start with the breath. The breath is the only thing true to the moment. This moment. The breath is ever-present; it's not rooted in the past, it's not pulled toward the future, it's not connected to fear, joy, or anything else. The breath is neutral, and it brings us back to a neutral space. The breath is always here and now, and it will always bring you back. It allows us to gently reset. Start with stillness, find the center of your being, where that is, and pause. Then imagine connecting down into the earth. I picture an actual anchor dropping out from the bottom of my tailbone (my root chakra) and anchoring into the center of the Earth – a grounding white supportive light in the middle of the planet that we can tap into at any time. From there, I begin to breathe, bringing that light up and into my body. (I like box breathing; *see page 41*.)

★ It helps if you touch something earthy – sit on the ground, touch a plant, hug a fucking tree, you know, the usual stuff. This will bring you back to your senses. And yes, I actually hug trees.

Shift Your State

This is about choosing how you want to feel. After I've centered myself, after I'm full of grounding white light, I feel my desired state. We anchor into it by visualizing with each breath that we have become that state. I believe it while I weave it (*see page 219*). I align my feelings and emotions with my desired outcome, as if I'm already there. Here and now. With each inhale, I bring more of this awareness into my field. With each exhale, I visualize my anchor getting deeper into the foundation. I literally energetically anchor into it.

Okay, but how do we find that feeling?

Think of a moment you felt so much love and gratitude for someone, or that moment the bank deposit hits on pay day. That's your baseline, then go bigger. Imagine it gets even better, so what shows up is better. If you base everything off a past experience you might hit that same ceiling. Go big, babe. You deserve it. Anchor into the energy. It's always there and available for you to tap into; you don't need to wait for pay day to feel paid. Feel more joy, find more joy. Feel more money, find more money. The more you feel it, the more life will reflect back a reason to feel it. The longer (and cleaner) you anchor into the energy, the sooner it shows up.

So what do you want to anchor into? Set your sails and get on with it. This won't only help stabilize you when the waves get rough, it'll help you navigate the present moment, and eventually dock in a whole new harbor.

Let's practice anchoring.

Energetic Boundaries

What's mine is not yours, and what's yours is not mine. It goes for food. It goes for shoes. And it also goes for energy. Honestly, I don't want what's yours, I've got enough on my own plate. And trust me, some of the ancestral shit I'm still clearing is not something you'd likely want to take on either (lol send help!). So, let's stay in our lanes, shall we?

Energetic boundaries help you understand where you end, and others begin. These boundaries can help protect your energy (*see page 168*), but while protection is about shielding you from others and external energies, boundaries are all about you. Boundaries are relational. Boundaries help teach others how they can interact with you. Boundaries help you regulate the energy you invest, how much you give, what you do, and what that exchange looks like. We need to learn how to set boundaries without fear or guilt. Boundaries can help us navigate our flow and interactions with others, and even with ourselves. And yes, you can betray your own boundaries, so watch for this.

You can use boundaries to teach others what is and isn't acceptable: 'Sorry, I don't take work calls after 5 p.m.' or 'No, I'm actually not available that evening.' You can use them to re-parent yourself, too. 'No more garlic bread, Chris' I say to myself, before asking the waiter to remove the piece I pretend I can't squeeze in. If you say no phone past 7 p.m., and bedtime by 10 p.m., then honor it. It builds a stronger frequency. You learn to trust yourself deeper. You protect yourself. It all amplifies, and your external world reflects that back. I find the better I am with my internal boundaries, the better I am with external ones.

Boundaries can be set with your spirit guides as well. Like spiritual office hours. There are moments where I'm driving and BOOM a flood of ideas or information about someone I know or a project I'm building comes rushing in while I'm cruising down the freeway and definitely not sitting on the beach with a pen and paper. So now what? Pull the vehicle over? No. Instead we can create a rhythm or an intentional opening, like a mini ceremony or ritual, that shows our guides, 'Hello, I'm available and I'm not about to end up in a ditch while receiving this.' Imagine being open, and sensitive, and psychic all day every day, maybe some of you are. That's not good. Don't wear that as a badge of honor. I see this a lot in my clients – 'I'm just SO sensitive, I feel everything!' Well, babe, you shouldn't. Don't glorify it. That's an energy leak and it's counterproductive. Set boundaries. Trust that if something major happens and your guides need to show up regardless, they will – especially if it's tied to your safety or a mega opportunity. Otherwise, set office hours. Set them at the office, set them at the altar, just set them. You're a human; you shouldn't be dancing in the other realms 24/7. You should be here.

So try it out. Experiment with something small if boundaries or speaking up make you nervous. Set boundaries with yourself, your guides, your boss, whoever. Set a bedtime. Set a garlic bread boundary, as hard as it can be. Take time to connect with your guides, and then intentionally disconnect. No evenings full of emails. Put your fucking phone down. Boundaries are about you taking care of you, so take care.

XO

How 'Bout No?

Okay, so lately every time my mind or ego wants to stress about something I can't control – especially if I'm slipping into victimhood – I'm catching myself and saying, 'How 'bout no?'

I'm honestly shocked at how nice life can be when we're not downward spiraling for sport.

Obviously, I'm down for shadow work, but I'm also at peace with not needing to excavate every part of me all the time. I'm okay with not diving into the deep end of the unheated pool every time I'm triggered. I'll float in the shallow end today, thanks. Any takers wanna lotion me up?

There's always something trying to make us feel less-than. There's always someone casting doubt. Sometimes the call is coming from inside the house... well, how 'bout no? I'm not fuckin' answering. Self-doubt? Insecurities? Old stories? Your projections? How 'bout no. I'm not interested in watering myself down so I can be more easily digestible. Don't even ask. The answer is no. How 'bout no?

This was a great tool in my last relationship when my hypervigilance would kick in. Where is he? What is he doing? I bet he's... HOW 'BOUT NO!? I would interrupt the pattern and take a few breaths. I would focus on something else – I'm not interested in looping through the same old shit anymore. It's exhausting living in the same nightmare over and over again. At some point we need to say no. Do you ever find yourself asking leading questions that look like you're asking one thing but really you're trying to get clarity on something else? How 'bout not doing that? Stop manipulating the conversation and just say what you wanna say (don't worry, babe, we all do it unconsciously). This is rooted in survival. Control the environment. How 'bout no? How 'bout more thrivey and less survivey? How 'bout surrender; how 'bout sitting with our own feelings instead of dragging someone else through them? Now that shit will save a relationship! How 'bout we don't get upset, or pick a fight or start drama when we feel the old pattern showing up?

Sorry traumatized psyche – not today. Sorry old habits, it ain't happening. More garlic bread? How 'bout yes? NO! I mean how 'bout no?! When you wanna do what you've always done, say Fuck it, how 'bout no? I'm doing the opposite.

'How 'bout no?' goes hand in hand with boundaries. It lets you decide what is and isn't coming with you into the next chapter. It's about choosing something different, in the moment. Responding instead of reacting. It helps repattern your mind by interrupting the learned behaviors and redirecting your energy elsewhere. After you say no, you can choose what to do with that energy. Experiment with it, it helps. Eventually, you can retrain your mind and focus on what matters. I know they say old dogs can't learn new tricks, but woof woof, bitch. Here we go.

Fuck This, Fuck That, Fuck It * one of my fave practices.

Lately I've been thinking about this Fuck It energy.

Fuck It – I'm just gonna say something.

Fuck It – I'm just going to do it and see what happens.

Fuck It – Let's try this out.

Fuck It energy is about action.

Move to Portugal. Buy a cabin in the woods. Host a dinner for your new neighbors. Book that trip. Fuck It. Why not?

What is your 'I wish I could'?

What if you said 'Fuck It'?

What if you just *did* it?

How can you work this into your life and actually apply it?

Take out your journal or wherever you write things down (*see Journaling on page 89*) and capture anything that comes to mind, no matter how absurd. Move to New Orleans and start giving ghost tours. It can be anything! I'm not saying you *have* to do it. I'm just saying Fuck It, let yourself dream. Experiment. Then pick one, say 'Fuck It' and gett'er done!

I know it can feel intimidating to book that solo trip and go swim with wild pigs, but I want you to at least start thinking about all the possibilities out there. You are the architect of your own life. You get to choose *you*. Wanna be a millionaire? Fuck It! Believe it while you weave it – I did! (*see page 219*).

Fuck It is about taking the leap, but every leap needs a foundation to jump from. And so, I present to you, the wildly liberating ancient art of saying, 'Fuck This'.

Fuck This

This is the release. It liberates you from what draining your energy. It purges the perceived responsibilities you take on that aren't actually yours; the shit that steals your time and energy. Not every argument is worth your energy. Not every invitation is aligned. 'No' is a complete sentence. Use it. This is about boundaries (*see Energetic Boundaries on page 175*). We say 'Fuck This' to the things that suck us dry (and not in a good way!). Fuck This job. Fuck This shitty friendship. Fuck This need to explain myself 24/7. 'Fuck This' is the point of honest recognition: something is costing too much of your time, energy, or money. Or all of the above. And you're done. It's not about rage, it's about clarity. So, go on. Have the audacity to say it: Fuck This! Say it again. Mean it. And walk the fuck away.

Fuck That

And now, please welcome to the stage (drumroll, please): Fuck That! Fuck That might be my favorite fuck (aside from the 'you-know-what' kinda fuck that is *definitely* everyone's favorite kinda fuck, wink wink, nudge

nudge). Fuck That is your key to rejecting and rebuking the bullshit. 'Balance is 50 percent work, 50 percent play.' Fuck That. I prefer a 20/80 split. Or 10/90. 'What's your dream job?' Fuck That, I don't dream of labor, babe. I want to flow with creative projects and make a fuck ton of cash. Fuck That invites you to break the rules that break you. Live your life on your own terms. If it keeps you trapped, Fuck That! Authority without integrity? Fuck That. Inheriting your parent's scarcity mindset or fear of being seen? FUCK THAT. It's not yours. Rebuke it. Then say Fuck This. I'm not doing this anymore. Then say Fuck It, and take that leap of faith in a whole new direction.

So there it is: Fuck This. Fuck That. Fuck It.

Now stick that in your back pocket and get out there and do whatever the fuck you want with it!

From Victim to Victory

Two years ago I thought I was entering a space of victory. I had made millions. I had tons of followers. I built Wheelhouse, a beautiful creative hub in Lisbon. Everything was expanding. All these people working together in pursuit of a shared vision. Wow! I made it!

But then my target of victory moved. I had to move it. My passion became a prison, and I needed a different definition of victory. I've been through the 'more money, more problems' whirlwind and I barely made it out alive. Let me tell you, it's real! Money brings more complicated relationships, for one. Money also amplifies everything. Now, I just want to sit in nature with goats. I want to be at peace with someone I love in a comfortable space surrounded by birds and trees. *(Read about the farmhouse on page 227.)*

In moments I wondered – what part of me even built Wheelhouse? My love for community was one driving force, that's for sure. But what other parts of me were present? Did I want to prove myself? Did I want more money? Did I want to show people I could do it on my own? What voices were really in my head and what was their driving force?

Maybe it was my North American programming – bigger, more! Maybe it was my soul calling me deeper into creation. It's such a beautiful container – so many visitors ask if I'll open another location. Why not offer it somewhere else? I'm not ruling it out, but I'm interested in examining my 'why?' I'm asking myself all the same questions I'm asking you. I'm walking the same road. When a desire is rooted in authenticity, think of how much more aligned it will be, how much more fruitful. So much of what drove me to build Wheelhouse was love, connection, and community, but there were definitely shadow aspects driving me as well, and through this process I learned more and more about those parts. Even your shadow aspects can contribute to creating beauty. And we all have them.

This is what's so beautiful about our inner journey of discovery: Our shadows contribute to the light. They are two sides of the same spectrum and always in service to one another. No light, no shadow – and the darkness shows us where our light begins. We, too, are like the rolling sunrise to sunset and evening to dawn, an ever-flowing experience moving through the spectrum of lightness to darkness, and back again.

I'm actively redefining what victory looks like for me, and you should too, but the only way to get there is to identify where you're too deeply rooted in an outdated idea of victory. And that idea of victory could be rooted in your wounding (and we are all wounded, to some degree). You might want to read about the Drama Triangle vs. Empowerment Dynamic *(see page 114)* to understand some of those dynamics and how they play out.

I have a friend who is caught in a victim mindset. He wears it like a badge. He needs everyone to know his story and seemingly has no interest in changing it, for now. He needs an entire mindset shift to really take a leap forward. Right now, he's simply not ready to let it all go. I can offer him the same techniques I'm offering you. I've offered that and much more, but you need to meet people where they're at. It's not my fault that he rejects my offers; in fact, it has nothing to do with me. You know that expression, 'You can lead a horse to water, but you can't make it drink'? My friend is that horse.

Know your audience. Stop trying to convince people. Pivot toward people who are ready and open and interested. They're primed for learning and expansion. You're not responsible for anyone else's journey from victim to victory. Sometimes, we can hold space for others *(see page 144)* but we have to remember we're not responsible for their choices. Understand what's yours and what isn't. Focus on what victory means to you. And accept that it's a moving target. Make adjustments as needed. You're allowed to do that.

 When we think about victimhood, we also need to get out of the competition of who's in more pain or who has it worse. Pain is relative. Suffering is subjective. Malcolm X once said, 'The most disrespected person in America is the Black woman. The most unprotected person in America is the Black woman. The most neglected person in America is the Black woman.' I could never claim to understand the experience he's describing, I'm simply acknowledging the statement because it holds weight – I say that based on conversations I've had with Black female friends and other members of the community, both Deaf and hearing. This exact pain isn't something I've experienced. Does that make it any less real for them? No. My lack of experience doesn't invalidate theirs just like their experience doesn't invalidate mine. There are undeniable, measurable layers of privilege woven deep into our society based on race, disability, culture, sexual orientation, etc. that need to be acknowledged and shifted. As someone benefitting from these privileges, I and others like me (cisgendered, able-bodied, white male-presenting individuals with access to education and healthcare, etc.) need to be aware of our impact and do what we can to bridge the gap for these communities, support them, and reconcile with the damage done by these systems and invisible structures.

It's also fair to say that people benefitting from that privilege carry their own unique pain. Does their pain unconsciously trickle down and impact others? Absolutely. Are these systems invisible and rooted deep in our psyche? Yes. *(Jump over to Decolonization of the Mind on*

page 199.) But when we get caught in the battle of who is in more pain, the lens unfortunately shifts from solution to defense. I've been friends with and worked alongside Deaf people, and those living with varying degrees of ability and disability, since I was 17 — I've seen some wild shit, but we can't get lost in who has it worse or who struggles more. And I know that's easy for me to say, I understand that's part of the argument. But let's not get consumed by the argument and let's look at solutions, as best we can. We're stronger together, and competition keeps us apart. If we perpetuate separateness these systems continue to win. Why? Because we're distracted; we're all looping through and re-experiencing our own version of 'victimhood' and these actions reinforce hate and competition and the cycle continues. We need to step out of this cycle, together. It's the only way forward. This starts with acknowledging the pain and systems and people that perpetuate it, and from there, we pivot and find solutions. But we can't do that if we're in a competition of who has it worse.

The sooner we say Fuck This *(see page 179)* and build new systems together, the sooner we all find victory. The sooner we have the audacity to put ourselves out there, share our stories, and learn from each other, the sooner we can co-create a reality we *all* can enjoy. But that takes balls, or whatever you have down there. It means trying something new, experimenting with new ideas, being vulnerable, and taking a chance on yourself and others. So what world do you want to create, and how can we create it together?

We're stronger together.

Keep Going

Wherever you find yourself, just keep going. Of course, if you need to stop for water, or take a few days to rest, or maybe a month off, then take it. But eventually, we get back on the horse, and we ride at dawn. You might find yourself in the messy middle, or maybe you finally landed on solid foundation, but at some point the messy middle will find you again.

Let me explain what I mean by the messy middle. It's that moment where things begin to change. We make a big decision, we have a peak experience or a moment of low lows, and things begin to recalibrate. It's the overlap, the in-between. Picture a Venn diagram where one circle is your old life, one circle is your new life, and you're smack dab in the middle, likely crying while trying to hold it all together. It feels like watching two movies simultaneously and trying to catch every detail – and no, I'm not talking about scrolling on your phone while watching *Love Is Blind*. I'm talking about you actively building a new life while juggling the old one (which might be a total shit show). It's about having two identities at once.

The messy middle is not easy. I've been there a few times and it doesn't get easier, but you can learn to recognize it and find ways to ground yourself to stay sane. It's important to know you're not failing and nothing is wrong.

You can feel confused, overwhelmed, stressed, and anxious, like things are unraveling (which you're grateful for; *see page 117*). You're so fucking exhausted by it all that you can't bear it any longer. It's like forward momentum without relief. At the same time, you can be so excited about the opportunities coming your way and inspired by what's new. Brick by brick, your new life is slowly but surely coming together. Yet you still feel tethered to the old one. Your old life feels familiar but unsafe; your new life feels safe but unfamiliar. Your nervous system doesn't know how to respond.

Find a pillow and scream or have a good car cry like me. The messy middle requires slow and steady containment, not speed. Be gentle on yourself. You need time to metabolize. Release and renewal are not easy things. It can take a long time to let go, integrate, and mature into the next version of ourselves. We're not caterpillars, it doesn't take 10–14 days for us to turn into a beautiful butterfly, though some days I do feel like a blob of goo waiting for my wings. But good things take time. Beyoncé wasn't built in a day.

So, wherever you are is exactly where you're meant to be. For now.

You won't be there forever. If it's good, enjoy it. If it's shit, stay hydrated. Anchor yourself, lean into your practices and your community, and eat grounding foods. You're almost there, babe. You might lose some hair along the way, but you'll survive. I promise. Be gentle with yourself, deepen your gratitude, and keep going.

Just keep going.

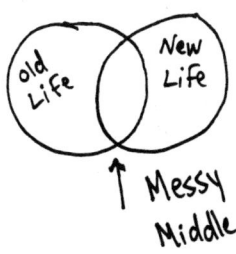

you can
doodle here, too!
here

Do **not** over-explain yourself to others.

Stop Rescuing people.

Say, "fuck this" and leave!

Make a list of all the ways you people-please. Then **stop.**

Set **one** strong boundary this month.

Let someone misunderstand you this week.

TRY SOMETHING NEW

Speak TF up!

Write a list of all the ways you betray yourself. Stop doing that.

* shut off your phone

Take a day off.

Say "No" five times this week.

♥ ♥ Treat yourself, babe. xoxo ♥

prioritize **your** needs!

Don't Go.

★ Make A Vision Board !!
$ ❀

Take up space.

Part 5

THE AUDACITY TO

DO The Damn **THING!**

(...or at least fucking try)

As you've probably gathered by now, life isn't totally random. It's a mirror reflecting back the energy and emotions we carry. Your auric field, energetic body, emotions and feelings, are part of the unseen layers working behind the scenes, shaping your reality and everyday experiences.

Every thought, feeling, and belief you repeat often enough eventually shows up in your physical reality one way or another – from mind to matter. So if you change those thoughts, feelings, and beliefs, it would only make sense that something else shows up, right? That is correct. Welcome to weaving a new web, Charlotte. Let's stop with this autopilot bullshit and intentionally create a life that's really worth living. It doesn't happen overnight, but it happens. Experiment with it. Have the audacity to hit pause and look around. How did you get here?

What you water grows. Where your focus goes, energy flows. Your beliefs become the blueprints for the world to construct itself around you, and sometimes it's a tedious build.

Sometimes it's full fucking liberation. So if reality is built with your mind, and if you've already built something, can you adjust the mind and build something else? Yea, babe. You can. Day by day, thought by thought, action by action.

You might know this and already be building something incredible (I love that for you!). Maybe you're living in a full-blown shit show. It's cool, we'll pivot. Maybe it's a bit of both – chaos with a heartbeat. Like a beautiful lover with terrible morning breath. Let's keep the good lay but lose the stench. Small adjustments every day is enough, don't rush it. See what methods work for you, set your goals, and take action. Your mind is already working, let's make it work for you. You deserve a great life and fresh breath!

Avoid Autopilot

A fish doesn't know it's in water until it's wet ass is floppin' around on dry land thinking, *What the fuck just happened!?* We, similarly, don't realize we're stuck in the mundane, same-old-shit kinda energy until one day we wake up and think – *What the fuck have I been doing?* Our habits, conversations, and routines can become mindless over time. With enough repetition we don't need to think about what we do, or why we do it. It's engrained in the mind and memorized by the body; we're on autopilot.

Have you ever driven home and realized you don't remember the route? Or stopped mid-shower wondering if you washed your hair yet? You completely zoned-out. Like going through the motions at work, day in, day out. It's like you're sleepwalking.

The good news? You can wake up.

We can rewire this default programming. Our ego (the self) enjoys predictability, but comfort creates a slippery slope into autopilot, and autopilot is the thief of our potential. When we're unconsciously taking a backseat on life, we're not intentionally creating it. You're not making choices. You might be alive, but you're not living. When we notice those autopilot moments, we take our control back. That's the point of this book: reclaiming choice. Choose to weave your life like a beautiful tapestry, not a crunchy bathmat on autopilot. Maybe first unravel a few things to create more space, but what a gift realizing you're the weaver. So, weave whatever TF you want.

To weave a life you love, you need to align the self with the soul. For most of us, it takes time to get there. When self and soul are on the same page, we find flow – doors open, people show up, opportunities expand. We weave our reality intentionally, it's not unconsciously woven for us, by us. Sometimes that means starting over. Sometimes, it's less dramatic. And I get it, maybe you're comfortable in your overpriced 33rd floor apartment in downtown Toronto bartending all night and smoking weed all day. Maybe you love that view, or have a great mattress, and a beautiful fig tree. Maybe it's a lot to give up, but trust me, it can get a whole lot better.

So is it worth letting it all go?

In short, yes. I'm sorry but an inconvenient truth is that our calling, our intuition, *is inconvenient*. It's easy to do what other people tell you to do. It's easy to stay in that same town with the same job and the same benefits. Shifting into a new life is gonna be hard for like three, six, maybe even 12 months while you throw yourself into re-discovery. You need time to explore, and sometimes that's uncomfortable, like growing pains. But I swear, I've done this before and I'll do it again, because every fucking time, I weave a life better than the last. *Every. Fucking. Time.* Like, mind-blowingly better. You need to trust your soul, your intuition, and your process, even when it's inconvenient. Even when it's uncomfortable for us, or those around us. Only after we jump will wings appear. And only then can we soar into a whole new world. Cue Aladdin.... *'Don't you dare close your eyes! A whole new world – HOLD YOUR BREATH IT GETS BETTER!!!...'* Can you tell I'm a gay 90's kid? Alright, Abu. Let's move on.

The moment it clicks that you're part of a world that's built to support a few at the top is pretty fucking upsetting. They had the audacity to force you into it without you even knowing. Zero consent. You might feel betrayed. Tricked. Robbed of your time, your energy, your money. That's because you were.

I was too.

Welcome to the club!

But there are other factors that have contributed to your default settings. Genetic coding, family history, expectations, childhood experiences, even our karma and dharma play into it *(see page 213)*. Before we can do anything about it, we have to understand we unconsciously agree to a lot of these things. We buy into the stories that shape us. We accept what others say, we accept what we were born into, as the only available option. Who we used to be, what we used to do, how we used to do it. We were on board with it, to some degree, for some time, and for some reason, and that's okay (self-forgiveness/compassion is key here). This all stems from our stories. And stories are just ideas and words that pass through our mind that we hold onto, and choose to believe. They are not the ultimate truth. As soon as we realize we're making choices based on our beliefs, and our beliefs are based on stories, and stories are connected to the thoughts we have about ourselves, others, and experiences, the sooner we can pivot. First we realize; then we release. Kinda like fishing – we catch the thought, and release it. We don't have to hold onto it, or believe it, we can let it go. We can do that through these supportive practices (and others, but I like these ones).

Supportive Practices

- Tapping (great for reprogramming the thought itself, so you catch better fish!)

- Shaking (helps get excess mental static/energy off the body)

- Sweating (heat built in the body can purify overthinking)

- Screaming (just a great fucking release)

The Audacity to Do the Damn Thing 197

- Crying (super cleansing and helps balance the emotional body)

- Laughing (the best medicine)

- Writing (putting it on paper creates more mental space)

These practices help move energy.

If nothing shifts, take more time doing the exercise or try combining a few until you're feeling less activated. Then, look around and see what's contributing to whatever is happening. If the cake sucks, change the recipe, right? When we get off autopilot we see choices that are right in front of us. We can adjust the ingredients of whatever we're cooking up and try something new.

You don't have to accept every hand you're dealt. Acknowledging where you're at helps you change directions, but if you wanna trade some cards, you don't need anyone's approval. Be the black sheep – Baa Baa, babe. If you're reading this book, you're probably already a misfit to some degree. You likely always knew there was something more, somewhere, and maybe felt like an outsider or that you didn't fit the mold. Me too.

Welcome home. All the little weirdos are welcome here.

Let's blow this popsicle stand and show the world what we've got.

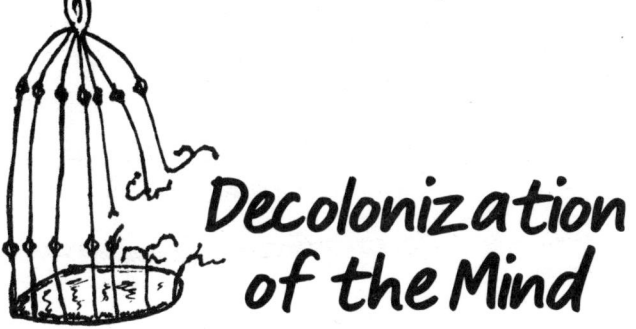

Decolonization of the Mind

To improve our mental, emotional, and spiritual health, sometimes we need to wipe the slate clean. I'm not here to lecture you on reconciliation or reparations – though both conversations hold real weight and deserve space. But I do want to gently draw your attention to something that's rarely discussed. When the generations before us robbed others of their culture, traditions, beauty, stories, art, language, and wisdom, they robbed us too. If you find yourself getting the urge to skip this chunk, don't. If it feels uninteresting to you, you likely need to hear it. When settlers first arrived, there was an attempt to sanitize the land, but they unknowingly sanitized themselves, and all of us, in the process.

We live in a world that has tried to erase and disempower Indigenous, Black, and other global cultures. In their attempt to eradicate others, they drained depth, color, and richness from all of us. I live in a world where my body and my mind carry a history that maintains inherited power and privilege. Those like me carry invisible tendencies and blind spots based on that inheritance. For the most part, white able-bodied people, men, financially stable families, people in a mainstream religion or culture, and citizens of powerful nations are privy to these privileges. Needless to say, Black, Indigenous, and People of Color (BIPOC), women, trans and non-binary people, disabled folks, poor or working-class people, those who have been displaced, homeless, or made into refugees, stateless people, or those in colonized regions, and so many others, do not share the same benefits.

 These systems are designed so that privilege remains invisible to those who have it. This way the power can be passed on through generations and kept from others. We don't tend to act if we remain unaware of how other groups are suffering.

Some people may look rich on paper, having unlimited resources and such, but many are poor in spirit. When we remove culture, people, and traditions, we remove the richness that makes life worth living. They didn't just destroy what belonged to others, they destroyed opportunities for collaboration, innovation, and creation. This world has not been shaped by all of us, and it shows. They didn't just fuck everyone else up, they fucked themselves up, too. They fucked it all up.

So, let's unfuck it.

Our inherited mindsets walk us through doors that we don't even see open. Half of these doors are traps I've alluded to in other parts of this book; the structures that keep us disempowered. But this is where we need to ask new questions: Who is benefitting from these stories? Why is hyper-independence celebrated? Who is really winning when we're fighting each other? We're stronger together. In every way. We need to seek guidance outside of dominant narratives, reclaim our own traditions, practices, and inner voices, while helping others reclaim theirs. We need community, nature, and spirit instead of more things that feed into profit, power, and rivalry.

We all benefit from decolonization – our minds open, our imagination expands. When everyone contributes creativity skyrockets. When we give people space to be who they are we, too, reclaim who we are. We liberate each other. The colonized mind is cluttered with rules, and fear, and binaries – we've all inherited this bullshit – unevenly, but undeniably.

I watched *Black Barbie: A Documentary* on Netflix and realized for decades Black children were handed white dolls and told they were beautiful while dolls in their own image were either nonexistent or distorted into caricatures. When asked which dolls were pretty and which were ugly, the kids almost always associated the white dolls with beauty and the black dolls with the lack of it. These children were internalizing whiteness as the standard and seeing themselves as less than. That's so fucked up. Now consider how many people have internalized how many narratives. All of us. It's just the narratives have different intentions.

You Should Watch It.

Historically, channels of mass media, like Hollywood, curate these narratives. With the trans community, for example, they cast trans people as predators or jokes (see: *Ace Ventura Pet Detective*). Onscreen it's entertainment, offscreen trans people are denied rights, healthcare, and basic safety. Or Indigenous Communities traditionally being portrayed as savages, mystical guides, or mascots. Their culture presented as exotic or primitive, while in reality their land is taken, the colonizers attempt to assimilate them, and their women and children are missing or murdered. Even larger bodies are typically cast as comedic sidekicks, or clumsy friends, with jokes made about their weight, while in real life they face discrimination in healthcare, jobs, and other areas.

Movies and television silently shape ideas about us all. White characters are often beautiful, robust, complex individuals, while others are simple, silent, side-lined, and supportive. These beliefs and behaviors are passed on through generations until someone decides to reshape the lens they're looking through.

That's what we're here to do. Reshape the lens. If you're in a position of privilege, don't play the savior. Don't beat yourself up, either – an emotional fallout is a natural reaction – shame, denial, survivor's guilt, defensiveness, overcompensation, grief. Experience what you need to, then buckle up *(see The Audacity to Feel it All on pages 31–101 and The Audacity to Let Go on pages 103–127)*. Allyship is needed. Do your own research, ask people what they need (don't assume), listen more than you speak, be accountable, and share your space/platform/microphone. Notice when you're taking up space that isn't yours to take. Abundance, expansion, and our highest expression all stem from inclusion, a mix of perspectives, and real connections.

This isn't about shame and this isn't just about making things right; this is an invitation for you to expand your mind into new paradigms that will, without doubt, invite new possibilities. Experiment with another lens. Dive deeper into the decolonization of mind and matter and expand your inner world – this isn't just about the past, it's about expanding into a healthier future for all of us.

Free your Mind

Harmony vs. Balance

You can only hold so much. If you're feeling burned-out, you need more rest, more play, and less on your to-do list. Burnout is rooted in obligation. It's hard to get burnout doing shit you love all day, it's the shit we don't love that drains us. Burnout is the result of pressure, not passion. Exhausted? Over it? Same, babe. To find your center again, you need harmony.

We've all been told we need balance but what if the idea of balance keeps us away from the balance they claim balance will bring? What we really need is harmony. Think about nature. Is it made up of 50 percent water and 50 percent earth? Is it perfectly balanced? No, babe, and you shouldn't be either. Roughly 71 percent of Earth is water. It's asymmetrical and dynamic, and that's why it works.

We need to harmonize all of our parts. Like water, we need flow, ease, and to surrender. Like fire, we need action, destruction, and expansion. A dance of co-creation. There's 'Fuck it, let's do this!' energy, and then there's rotting for five hours on your couch. There's joyful connection and there's 'Everyone get the fuck away from me.' There are moments of planning and moments of impulse. Balance isn't real or attainable. Fuck balance. Find harmony.

Like a traditional scale that only finds center with equal weight on both sides, balance demands perfection. Harmony provides flexibility. I don't want a work/life balance that's an equal split. I wanna work five hours a week and enjoy the rest of my time. I'm not there yet but I'm getting closer and trust me, it's possible. Are you gonna be laying on your deathbed thinking, *I'm so grateful half my time was billable hours?* I really fucking hope not. We don't sleep 12 out of 24 hours a day. We don't eat equal portions of everything on our plate. We don't hang out with each friend for exactly one hour and set a timer to make sure we're not late for the next one. You're not supposed to be balanced. You're not a fuckin' flamingo.

Harmony is unique to each of us. It's about coherence and attunement to our own needs. We're multi-faceted beings. Our desire to play, our commitments to work. Our masculine and feminine expressions. Our inner child and adult self. Our choices need to be rooted in both our responsibilities and values. Sometimes you need to go, go, go. Sometimes you need to sit your ass down. Create space for all of it.

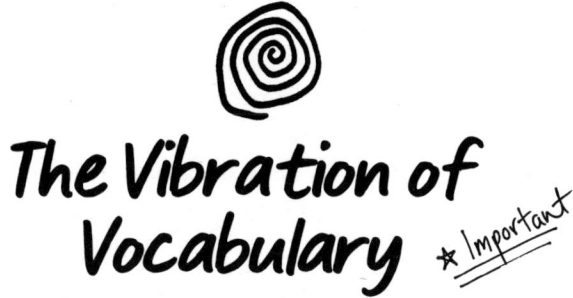

The Vibration of Vocabulary *Important

Vocabulary carries vibration, so be aware of how you speak. Your thoughts and words impact your life and those around you. When I started taking this seriously, things seriously shifted. There's a few cool things I noticed: What we say shapes our reality, but it also reveals the deeper layers of what we think about ourselves and the world around us. I noticed that certain words have specific energetic charges to them – those charges reveal our relationship with that word and the energy behind it. I really want this to land, so experiment with me here for a second. Try this out.

Try this →

Pause for a minute. Take a few slow, deep breaths. Calm down, center yourself, then continue reading.

Seriously, pause and take a deep breath – it's important for this next part.

If you feel grounded, if you feel a sense of calm and neutrality, notice how you feel when you read this:

You're Words Shape Your Reality.

Did you notice the spelling error? How did you feel reading it? What happened in your mind or your body? Did your energy shift from neutral to something else? Maybe judgment? *He's writing a book and he doesn't know the difference between you're and your?* I presented this during a keynote with a slideshow in front of like 300 people and someone in the audience literally gasped out loud.

I hope you noticed a shift when you saw that error and made whatever judgment or thought whatever thought. The whole point I'm making is when a thought or a judgment shows up, regardless of what it's about, it influences your energy. Imagine if you're experiencing erratic thoughts or talking poorly to yourself all day. Or judging others. If you're gossiping instead of dreaming. If you're freaking out instead of chilling out. Your energy, even your body, is responding. Each word holds a frequency, and those frequencies affect our feelings, and our feelings affects what we create. And we're creating our reality. It's all connected.

Your vocabulary also reveals where you have unconscious ideas or fears about a specific something. Have you ever been in a conversation where things go from 0–100 REAL QUICK? You say something and trigger the shit outta someone? I called someone 'babe' once and they literally stopped our conversation and told me to never call them that because it was condescending. *Sure, babe.* Apparently there's some unresolved issues goin' on there because I wasn't being condescending and I call everyone except my mom babe, so I'm pretty sure that wasn't on me, but obviously I stopped. She really didn't like sweetie either.

I'm kidding – I'm not intentionally an asshole so I apologized, but my point is the word itself revealed something. A trigger *(read about Triggers on page 71)*. So, what triggers you? What words trigger what emotions? What vocabulary feels charged for you, and why?

Let's find out.

ok, now try this

Triggering Words

Take another minute to center yourself. Take a few deep breaths, then come back and try this.

Find a neutral mind and body before moving on. Once you feel calm, slowly read each word and notice which ones activate something – what emotion or feeling comes up? Expansion or contraction? Resistance? Joy? Okay, begin.

Mom	Money	Religion	Masturbation
Love	Dying	Fame	Porn
Health	Colonization	Family	Cancer
Addiction	God	Sex	Greed
Dreaming	Control	Failure	Power
Abortion	Manipulation	Shame	Orgasm

How'd you do? There's no right or wrong way to feel – it's simply an exercise to observe what words might have a charge to them. If you want, ask yourself why. I chose some taboo topics on purpose. I noticed my own charge with some words as I typed them. I felt empathy, expansion, even a little cringe. Whenever you had an 'unpleasant' charge – maybe the word 'masturbation' felt weird – then there's likely a story there. Something under the surface. This applies to all words and can be a dangerous thing. Sun Tzu, in *The Art of War*, says that 'if you can control your opponent's emotions, you can control the battle,' and honestly that shit lands. It's important to know yourself, and what triggers you. But why does this happen?

My dad has lived with cancer for years. His dad died of cancer (shout out to Papa). I'm noticing as I type this that there's no real 'charge' to it anymore, but that took work. For a long time the word 'Cancer' freaked me TF out. I had internalized this idea that their story was my story. That 'I was next.' With so much unprocessed grief, fear, and anxiety still in my body, I carried stories and ideas that I created through a limited lens. One word could throw my whole nervous system into overreaction. Like all stories, I would find evidence to support it, and get lost in the spiral.

We can re-charge these words. Or, you can choose to avoid certain words for now. If you felt discouraged reading the word 'Dreams' maybe there's some gunk you need to clean out. If the word 'sex' made you feel shame or cringe, reclaiming your sexual power may be needed.

Maybe you're triggered when people talk about money, or when they say your ex's name. There's a story there. Maybe pain. That story has a script and that script has words. Those words 'mean something' to you. One word can tell a whole story. That story has as assumed outcome. That outcome may be expansive or contractive depending on how you subconsciously relate to that word. Either way, that word means something to you.

If you're looking for expansion, examine the limitations hidden in your vocabulary. This isn't just about the words we hear, but the words we use. Love means something different to all of us. So does work, or play, rest, and liberation. We need to redefine and recharge our vocabulary with meaning that creates positive impact. We can choose our words selectively and charge our words intentionally. We may even need to discharge certain words.

You get to choose what those words mean for you. You *can* recharge your vocabulary. I've done it. I've re-charged words so they don't carry the same weight they used to. I've re-assigned meaning and realigned myself with old words in new ways. Now these words are empowering instead of triggering. Our vocabulary reveals what we think about ourselves, and what we think is possible. I used to refer to a massage as a treatment, but I stopped because it sounds like I'm treating an ailment. For me, it felt off, so I got away from that word altogether. Now I'll say I'm going for a massage, or to pamper myself. You know? Somethin' cute. Sometimes I say, 'body work,' or whatever; I use a word that intentionally reflects something positive to me. There's well-established evidence proving that word choice literally changes our physiology and alters our nervous system. Now, when I'm about to say something like, 'I'm sick and tired' of something, I catch myself and I say, 'I'm over it' instead. Why would I want to claim being sick and tired? Our language shapes our reality. It's no shock that my Deaf friends hate being called Hearing Impaired. It's not an impairment and it's offensive to assume that they're dysfunctional. They are Deaf with a capital D. No need to 'fix them.' Let's fix our language. Let's see where we trap or liberate ourselves, and others, through the vibration of our vocabulary.

Vibration of Vocabulary

Dreaming and Imagination

Your dreams are your assignments – they pull you and nudge you into the direction of your highest expression. These can be literal dreams, the kind you have while you're asleep, or figurative dreams, like unburdening yourself from all responsibilities, moving to a farm, and becoming a toothless 93-year-old shepherd. Maybe that's just me idolizing my neighbor, but a boy can dream!

Your dreams might not make sense to other people. When I told my mom I was gonna quit my job and become a tarot card reader she almost shit herself. Now, she's on a team that helps manage my finances and shits herself for another reason – she didn't know it was possible to generate millions of dollars doing this. And honestly, neither did I. But something, somewhere did – and that's why I dreamed about it.

Wheelhouse was another dream I manifested. My space here in Lisbon – a space to create, connect, rest, and recover. We host community events and workshops. There's a salt cave, and a tea lounge. There's a fuckin' fairy house in my café garden. And I dreamed it all up! Of course, teamwork makes the dream work. But someone's gotta plant the seed. Your dream is like a map from your Future Self (read Bending Time on page 25). It's an invisible compass helping navigate your next move. We all have our own unique path, our own unique dreams, and when we act on them, we help reshape and rebuild the world in our own little way. By stepping into our dream life, we inspire others to do the same. By having the audacity to be who we really are, and go after what we really want, we heal ourselves and each other. Authenticity invites others to be authentic. It builds trust, community, and opportunity for leadership and collaboration.

Do you know Stefani Germanotta? She dreamed of being Lady Gaga. I remember the first time I heard 'Born This Way.' Sitting at George Brown College, learning how to interpret ASL, and my queer friend ran up to me looking noticeably shook. *You need to see this*, they said. So, I watched the music video and it blew my fucking mind. I felt so seen by a stranger on the internet. I felt included, accepted, and considered. I know it may sound dramatic, but that moment changed something in me. Watching her in her full expression, living her dream, inspired me to live mine. It felt safer being authentic – it was permission to show up as I am. I hope this book inspires you to come as you are. That moment helped me live my own dream, I hope this, too, helps you live *yours*. At least have the audacity to try. Experiment. If you take a wrong turn, pivot.

The path reveals itself as you walk it.

Think of the Hermit card in the classic tarot deck. He has a lantern that illuminates only the next step or two. He doesn't know how to get there, but he knows where he's going – toward his vision. He, too, is following a dream.

Manifesting your vision, dream weaving your reality, requires play and discovery. Your imagination reveals what's possible, but play is the practice that actualizes it. Gaga's kooky costumes – do you think those came from taking herself too seriously? Fuck no. She had fun with it, babe. Everything flows from fun. Everything you see was once an idea that someone played with, until it took its final form. The book you're holding. The underwear you're wearing, if you're wearing any at all.

Even the medication you take. Someone dreamed that up. Everyone dreams but few have the audacity to make their dream a reality. Your dreams have been delivered to you by divine design, so get out there and make it happen. Maybe you're the next Lady Gaga.

Let's Dream BIGGER

Karma, Dharma, and Energetic Echoes

Karma is not a scorecard.

I always thought Karma was like tit for tat. You did X now you get X. You put Y into motion, now Y comes back. I don't believe this anymore, not because I'm avoidant, but because I really don't believe God, Allah, the Universe, Creator, or whatever you want to call 'It' enjoys punishing us. I've done a lot of work around punishment. Releasing the idea that we must be shamed, or guilted, or harmed into learning. I've learned that way, and I've learned that's not the only way to learn.

Now, I see that Karma is more likely responding to your frequency and vibration. What you 'do' within that vibration will obviously rebound back to you and attract consequences aligned with those decisions, but the intricate energetic design of this unseen world is not that simple. Without gaslighting yourself, if you truly learned something from a misstep – if something shifted, and you truly integrated your lessons, and your frequency then expands into a new vibration, I don't believe you're still a vibrational match for that misstep to come back around and 'find you.' Karma is not hunting you down. It's an energetic match, not a debt. It's a reflection of your energetic state, not a direct give and get.

When you *really* shift your vibration, purge old beliefs, clear out shame and self-sacrifice, and dissolve any deeply rooted ideas and fears, you're literally rewiring yourself and reclaiming your autonomy, you're repatterning your mind, shifting your energy field, and aligning with a new frequency. You can maintain that frequency through action and anchoring *(read about Anchoring on page 171)*. Your reality then shifts and things begin to change. Whatever is not a vibrational match no longer aligns with you. Maybe that Karma will find you in another life, at a point when you're a vibrational match for it, but in this lifetime, when you truly shift your vibration, thoughts, emotions, and choices, you enter a different reality, and that karma may not be aligned with it. Imagine someone trying to find you but you've taken an elevator to another floor. This is not an excuse to harm others and then try to shift your way out of the consequences – it doesn't work like that. But when you truly enter a new paradigm, the cause-and-effect chain resets, to some degree, and begins anew. If shame, guilt, and fear remain in your energy field, then you're partially tethered to the past, and technically still a match. That's the entry point for the Karmic return. But if you've cleared the energetic echoes of the past, cut the cords, integrated the learning and appropriately matured your consciousness, then there's nothing left to magnetize the old life back toward you. Congrats – you've cleaned shit up. Ever notice how some people just disappear forever? Like you knew them, so intimately, then one day you split up and somehow never see them again, even if you're in the same city? It's because you're operating in two different dimensions. You've shifted your field and they're no longer a match.

Let's look at Dharma.

Dharma is your service to the world. Your unique personal path and offerings. Naturally, it includes some of the bullshit that's here to shape you, the challenges you signed up for on a soul-level, but it's ultimately in service of your highest expression.

Your service is often rooted in your divine play. I'm not talking about Leela, which translates from Sanskrit more directly to 'Divine Play' like the cosmic game of life – spontaneous, creative, no real need for rigidity or force. I'm talking about living through our inner child. When we play, we find flow, and in our flow we find service. When we actualize our service and walk the path of our divine work, I believe we have found more alignment with our Dharma, our sacred duty. Dharma is like the evolution we came here to experience; the good and the bad. This opens doors to opportunity and expansion *(I talk about this more in Activating Abundance on page 246)*, but it also invites challenging moments. Someone can be aligned with their Dharma and be void of moral purity. I believe Dharma is not about positivity, it's about authenticity, and some people are authentic assholes. Have you ever wondered how people do terrible things still find 'success'? Maybe their Dharma triggers big lessons. I believe Dharma is neutral and connected to inner nature – even if that inner nature creates some chaos. This isn't an invitation to be a dick; it's an attempt at understanding how the darkness in this world can still serve the light. It all has purpose. We don't have to admire the impact to recognize the alignment. Some paths are helpful, some harmful, but they all contribute to shaping humanity, nonetheless.

Both Karma and Dharma can include Energetic Echoes. These are lingering vibrations or energies that spill over from past experiences, past events, even lifetimes. Have you ever met someone who's afraid of water, or dogs, or something random they can't quite explain? It may be an echo from another lifetime. Their soul remembers, their ego does not. Echoes can be good and bad. Good echoes carry joy, maybe a memory from childhood, or a talent that shows up out of nowhere – like the first time you do something and it feels familiar. Your soul remembers. Bad echoes can keep us stuck in fear, shame, or guilt. Stories that haven't been resolved can echo from our past and influence our moods or drive our decisions. This can happen long after we thought we'd processed something. This is why Cord Cutting *(see page 122)* is so important. The better we clean our wounds, the fewer echoes we have and the better we can manage them.

[handwritten margin note: ★ Spill over from past lifetimes]

Stop Manifesting (and Why It Doesn't Work)

Manifestation is such a buzzword.

I'm sure you've heard it all while scrollin' through Instagram but some of this bullshit keeps you stuck like a truck tire in mud.

'But Chris, you've manifested this book, your dream home, and millions of dollars...'

Yeah, babe, and you can too!

I *manifested* it. **Past tense.**

It has arrived, it is here, it has *manifested*, that's correct, and I'll happily use the word while describing the result of something I've done. Our words help shape our reality *(read The Vibration of Vocabulary on page 205)*. My issue is with the word 'manifesting' – it carries this subtle cue that we're still without something. It's passive, like we're waiting for something to show up. The more energy you put into waiting for something to show up, the more resistance and distance you create between you and the thing you're waiting for. When we focus on separation, we wait longer. If you're talking about manifesting it, you're affirming it hasn't manifested.

You claim it remains absent. Command it here, now. Believe it while you weave it. Act as if you already have it – anchor into the energy (read about Anchoring on page 171). Stop waiting for something to give you that feeling. Stop waiting for it (or them) to show up. Instead, feel the feeling now, as if it's already manifested. Align your actions and emotions and the Universe will deliver. When it's a vibrational match, it'll be there.

Instead, try 'co-creating.' We're creating something in real time with the Universe as it presents us with opportunities and results. It's a dance. As things naturally unfold, opportunities arrive, results manifest, and reality takes form in a way that matches our emotional state. Because we're a vibrational match, not because we're chasing it down.

It's like talking about who you're becoming. Who you're becoming is rooted in recognizing who you currently are *not*, because you are *becoming them*. You need to *be* now what you wish to become. Don't fake it 'til you make it – there's nothing fake going on here. When we are who we want to be, energetically, the 'new you' naturally comes into being. Stop trying to become something; be it.

'How can I be someone I'm not?'

You only doubt who you are because part of you thinks you need external confirmation before something can be true; but it works the other way around.

Affirming the truth of who you are is what bends reality to reflect that.

When we speak from the gap we prolong the gap. If we're always *healing something*, there's an implied idea that we're *still broken*, perpetuating our endless journey to be whole again. We remain fragmented. Close the gap, speak from the place you wish to be. Command what you want. Believe it. Be it.

Try it. Not for one day – commit. Try it for 90 days and see what shifts; it's important we build momentum. Believe it while you weave it.

Believe It While You Weave It

I always used to say 'Fake it 'til you make it' but then I realized that there's an energy of *This isn't real* woven into that. The truth is, we aren't faking it. Energetically, it's very real. So, now I say, 'Believe it while you weave it,' and I love this so much more. I've done this in the past, 'faked it' and actually made it, but it took a lot longer and a lot more fuckin' energy. Faking it is a performance. You're wearing a mask, playing a role, trying to convince yourself and the audience that you know WTF you're doing. When we're faking something we're suppressing how we really feel, trying our best not to slip up, and lying to ourselves and everyone else.

Believing in something liberates you from all that bullshit. You're not acting, you're aligned. We're stabilized by trust. We're anchored into our truth and living as our future self. We close the gap. There is no doubt.

Ten years ago I was driving a 2003 janky-ass Ford Focus, likely running on fumes, with a side mirror duct taped to the door and an AC unit that pumped hot engine air at you. My wonky armrest was as stable as my bank account at the time, pretty fuckin' wobbly and panicked. I couldn't afford anything outside of surviving (and drinking and smoking my stress away). I'd spend what's left of my paycheck on a $200 cellphone bill and a sad dinner. While crying into my noodles, I'd walk in circles saying 'I'm a millionaire. I'm a millionaire. This is chump change! I'm so fucking rich and grateful for the money that flows effortlessly toward me.'

Were those millions in my account? Not yet. My reality was still spicy ramen. But my energetic reality told a different story. I would pause with the panic, cry my ass off, then anchor back into the energy I wanted to experience. I walked around fancy neighborhoods to catch the vibe. I'd go to Gucci, try something on, and say 'I'll be back.' Guess who waltzed back in there and also bought a wardrobe for their dog?? I also popped into Louis Vuitton and snagged a pair of their Millionaire Glasses – Google them. That's some expensive-ass face plastic, but wow.

You need to believe it while you weave it. You gotta look beyond the duct tape and noodles and trust there's a version of you who has what you want. Be them. Hold the vibration and close the gap *(read Stop Manifesting page 216)*. Whether it's love, money, health, a Gucci raincoat for your dog, hold the frequency of having it.

Be grateful you have it and the Universe will deliver something to be grateful for.

Esther Hicks is an O.G. Badass Teacher who describes our vortex well – the force that attracts our experiences. WARNING: It also attracts the bad. Anxious thoughts? You're worshipping the problem. More problems manifest. Focusing on lack? More scarcity.

Our focus builds momentum. Momentum builds force. Imagine the force of a tornado sucking everything in around it. Our vortex pulls in the world that's built around us. More focus, more momentum, more force for creation (or destruction). It works for us and against us, so it's important that we build momentum intentionally – meditate at the same time, every day, if you can. Move your body, hold your boundaries, keep your energy clean and anchored into the outcome. Believe you're already there, build momentum, and fuel your vortex with your focus.

Affirmations

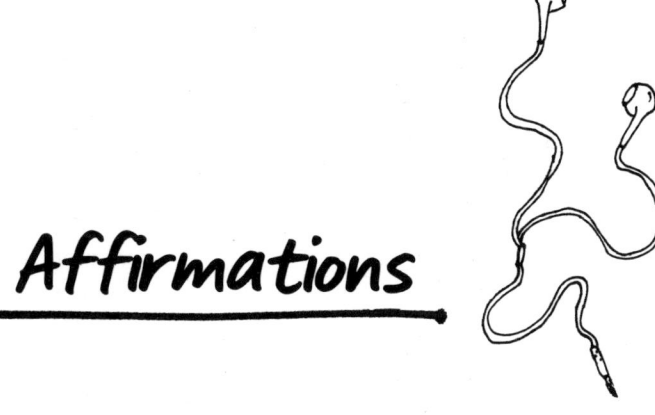

I don't love affirmations, but I do them and they work. Simple, repetitive, intentional statements impact your energy, redirect your mind, and shift your reality. They do.

Biologically speaking, the neuroplasticity in your brain gets rewired through repetition, and over time these ideas about yourself become hardwired and easier to access. We convince ourselves of something. Your brain's filter (the Reticular Activating System) looks for proof to support our beliefs and expectations. It's literally the same system that's stressing you the fuck out. It convinces us that we're not as cute as we used to be, or that muffin tops aren't adorable. Listen, if we're all loving this dad bod trend then I think we can gift ourselves a lil' cushion for the pushin', am I right?

Affirmations help prime us for an experience. Like when we're painting, we prime first so the paint sticks better. Prime yourself to receive an experience by experiencing the thoughts and feelings of it first, and let your brain seek out the evidence *(read Believe It While You Weave It on page 219)*.

Affirmations are equal parts woo-woo spirituality and wow-wow science. Your brain naturally builds new neuro pathways, seeking out evidence to support repeated ideas – just tell it what to look for. Sometimes I stare in the mirror repeating something to myself, other times I record my own affirmations. I put a cute lil' solfeggio frequency behind it, and I listen in the morning and before bed. THAT SHIT WORKS.

Affirmations Pointers

1. Speak confidently in present tense – 'I am rich.' Not, 'I might be rich one day.'

2. Don't go so big that your nervous system rejects the idea. Expand into realistic possibility and when you're comfortable there, go further. Baby steps work too.

3. Obsession attracts lack and distortion, consistency builds momentum. Don't fixate on your affirmations. Spend some time practicing, then surrender and move on.

4. Believe it while you weave it, don't fake it 'til you make it *(read page 219)*.

5. Words without action is a losing battle. Embody what you're saying. Say it. Be it. Do it. That's called integrity.

6. Have fun with it and celebrate any evidence you find along the way!

Experiment with this for 90 days and report back. May the force be with you.

Mantras

Time for a little *Ommmmmmmmm*.

Mantras are like affirmations that went to the gym and got fucking jacked. They're rhythmic, vibrational chants that pulse through your breath and body and they're insanely helpful at shifting our energetic state, rewiring our subconscious, focusing attention, and aligning our frequency with a desired vibration. I absolutely love Mantras. There are so many deities and energies we can connect with through mantras and if you're like me (Pisces in the 6th House) getting that rhythm, vibration, and practice INTO the body is literally life changing.

The vibratory nature of sound calms the nervous system and settles our energy field. It quite literally reduces your heart rate and hormonal stress markers helping you shift from fight or flight into a parasympathetic dominant state. Mantras take this one step further. By producing vibrations in the vocal cords and back of the throat, as we do when chanting mantras, we stimulate the vagus nerve – the main component of the parasympathetic nervous system – and naturally bring the body back to a regulated state. Yes, a little *Ommm* can go a long way in helping you land in a well-rested, centered state of mind and body, so, ummm, why would you not?

Mantras ground us, protect us, expand us, depending on our intention. Even mantras we don't understand turn certain 'keys' in the body. These ancient codes help us enter new states of consciousness, open us up to new ideas, and activate energies in our field. Repetition bypasses the logical mind, and our heart rate, breath, and brainwaves synchronize, dropping us into a calmer state. This amplifies mind and heart coherence. This process activates our toroidal field leading to clean and clear manifestations *(check out Your Magnetic Mind on page 60)*. Mantras clear distortions and ground us back in trust. They create space for liminal possibilities and help us intentionally broadcast a signal out to the Universe. They recode and clean our energy field. Mantras changed my life. Please experiment with it and let it change yours.

Synchronicities

While writing this book, Anna and I kept finding white feathers everywhere! In my car. On my cat's tail. One floated through the fucking window at the bagel shop and we both cried. (We cry a lot at Rhodo Bagel and not just because their barely baked gooey chocolate chip cookie is so good.) The feathers affirmed something. Presence. A quiet 'hello'. They let us know we're in the right place at the right time. It's like a wink from your guides letting you know you're on track. A love letter from the Universe.

What should you do in these moments? Pause. Take a second and say thank you. The more gratitude we have for the presence of our guides, the more they show up. These moments remind us that we're in alignment. They remind us it's a co-creation. If you find a lucky penny, don't scoff at it. Grab it! That's the point of the penny. How dare you scoff at a cute lil' penny tryna brighten up your day? Why would the Universe bring you millions of dollars if you refuse to accept a single penny? Broke-ass bitch, it don't make no sense.

I found a dime in Italy once and I cried. Now you're probably thinking *This guy is not okay...* and honestly, that's debatable, but I was so grateful for the dime, for the message, for what it represented at a time when I was in serious need of a sign. What the Universe was saying to me through that dirty little parking lot dime was, 'I've gotchu, boo. You're not alone. We hear you, we're workin' on it, and we're always with you, even when you think we're not. Trust the process.'

Does the process know we're trusting it?

Sometimes, we gotta just believe it while we weave it, babe. You're guides are workin' behind the scenes – say thanks for the dime and surrender to the process.

The pennies, the feathers, the 5:55 you catch on the microwave before heating up your pizza – they remind us there is something greater guiding us. Acknowledge the signs and be grateful, but don't turn everything into a synchronicity. I've done that and it's rooted in control. Synchronicities feels different. It's a deeper knowing, a moment of confirmation. It's a line in a song or a stranger's perfect comment. It's effortless and spontaneous. It arrives because you're in flow, not because you're seeking it out.

Sometimes you step in dog shit, and it doesn't mean 'they're not the one.' *Sometimes it does.* How relevant does the moment feel?

Only you know how important that moment was. Were you thinking, *I don't wanna work here anymore* when a white feather blew into your window and landed on your desk? Were you contemplating a trip to France and then spotted a stranger with a baguette pokin' out the top of their *JUST DO IT!* Nike bag? That's probably a sign. So keep an eye out for all the ways the Universe is speaking to you. But don't obsess. Real synchronicities aren't a dime a dozen, but sometimes a dime really is a sign.

This is your sign to scan this QR Code

The Farm

I wanted to buy a farm in Portugal. I wanted to slow down and shift gears for a minute. I found one I thought it was mine, then the deal went into limbo. Someone else made an offer and I felt like I was losing my house. The bank kept giving me issues with the mortgage application and I started spiraling – this *has* to be the house! I was freaking out and doing everything I could to hold on as tightly as possible. I was NOT losing this house!

I lost the house.

But I did find out what was really going on with me, so that's good. See, the house was amazing. It was big enough for the goats I wanted, it had a pool, imported Moroccan doorframes, vaulted ceilings, and, of course, crystals all over the place. It even had a lil' fountain that said 'Hakuna Matata' like in *The Lion King* (my favorite fucking movie, are you kidding me??). On my second visit I brought flowers as a 'thank you.'

I projected onto that house everything I wanted to feel once I had it, that was the problem. I thought I needed that house and if I'm sitting in the energy of need – the energy of being without something – then I'm in the vibration of lack. And that creates more lack. Yes, there were signs and synchronicities, but I was projecting onto those signs and synchronicities that this was *the* house, when really they were saying *this house is trying to teach you something.* And teach me it did. To receive something, you must be an energetic match. I first need to find peace, and then the

peaceful house will find me. Everything is an extension of our own energy. As within, so without.

I realized later that the flower offering was inauthentic. It was about control. Like a dog pissing on a bush, I was marking my territory. I was trying to manipulate the energy. Not cool. Didn't work.

As the deal fell through I let go of all expectations. I dropped the pressure. I played more; I took it all less seriously. I don't want a home that's an extension of control and manipulation, I want ease and flow. I embodied the energy I wanted to experience in that space. I reconnected with nature, slowed down, and recharged. I found more peace and gratitude in my current home. I remained open and gently seeking; I wasn't frantically searching. I changed my inner world without waiting for the outer world to reflect that.

Then – BOOM! Like when Dorothy stole that bitch's shoes, this house dropped right on my motherfuckin' lap. When I tell you this house was mind-blowing, I don't say it lightly. Made entirely of wood and stone, a river runs through the property feeding lush gardens and rolling hills of cork and olive trees. When I first entered the house, I felt it as a true extension of myself. I wasn't projecting onto it what I wanted it to be. I surrendered control and gently witnessed myself exploring it. Like swimming in familiar water, this house felt different. It was mirroring back to me what I wanted, but this didn't HAVE to be the one. I wasn't grasping at it, I was almost floating through it, as if the river outside was carrying me from one room to the next. I noticed the difference in my energy field. I was calmly observing the energy in the space and seeing how aligned it felt. I stepped into the garage alone and just started weeping with gratitude. *This is it.* This is the vibe, this is the type of home I want. I'm literally in the energy of it. If it's mine, beautiful, I am open to receiving it. If not, without doubt I'm getting closer. It just manifested before my eyes.

In part, those tears were because I found a house that felt truly aligned, but more importantly, I realized that energy, that peace and serenity, is something I had finally cultivated internally. And that's why this house showed up. This house was an extension of my energy. It revealed to me who I've become, and those tears acknowledge my arrival.

It's like dating when your life's a mess – you attract someone equally as messy. Sometimes, if you're both equipped, you can climb out of the mess together, but nine times out of ten the relationship fails. Why? You weren't even sure WTF you were doing at the time, and you thought dating would solve your problems? After the honeymoon phase wears off, the relationship just amplifies all the wounded parts that still need attention.

We attract what we are. ✸

With the farmhouse search, something clicked. I wanted peace, but I was frantic. I wanted serenity, but I was panicking. It wasn't until I stopped trying to control the outcome and focused on fine-tuning my energy that the Universe brought me something 1,000 times better.

How lucky we are to not get what we think we want.

The Universe always has something better up its sleeve. Anchor your energy. Cultivate the feelings. Stop waiting for something external to make you feel the way you want to feel and start feeling it now. Build momentum *(see page 219)*. Decide what you want and go after it. I want ducks and ponds. I don't want to multitask anymore. I don't want the American Dream – I want the Portuguese, goats by the river, slow living kinda dream, at least for now. Someone once said, 'In Italy, if you have a successful restaurant, you take time off. In America, if you have a successful restaurant, you start a franchise.' Well, as of now, I don't want a fucking franchise. And I don't wanna feel bad about not wanting more.

Purpose and Priorities

Whatever you're praying for, I hope you find it. And I hope in the gentlest way possible, if you find that you want something simpler, you pivot with ease and grace. I pray that you get there as quickly as possible, without burning the candle at both ends. I pray you don't waste millions of dollars on whatever you think you need to be bigger and better and brighter. I pray you can define what success truly means to you before you chase after someone else's definition of it.

Follow your heart. Keep it simple. Calm your mind, know your shadows, and prioritize self care. Don't let your fears, or the need to prove yourself, run the show. Don't overextend yourself. Growth without boundaries is destructive. Don't sacrifice yourself for your service. You may lose your joy, your play, your excitement for life. You may lose the connection to your inner child, and your sense of wonder. You might find yourself in a place so dark you forget the light exists. Like you're drowning in your dreams and your passion became a prison. I hope you never look back and ask yourself why you spent so much time on things that don't really matter. I'm telling you, it's not fucking worth it.

Get your priorities in check. What's important to you? Make time for that and protect it at all costs.

Don't chase love, validation, or money. Money can't provide purpose. It can only amplify it. If you're aligned, money fuels and expands that alignment. If you're lost, money buys more shit to get lost in.

We need purpose. Our purpose helps shape our priorities. Our priorities are like pillars that anchor us into our values. With alignment like that, we become a magnet – opportunities, love, and money flow into our life in a way that amplifies our expression instead of drowning us out.

When finding your purpose, take it slow, and get clear on what matters. Get intentional about what you're building. Identify your pillars. I learned the hard way but I'm cleaning it up. With a few priorities you could avoid the shit show altogether.

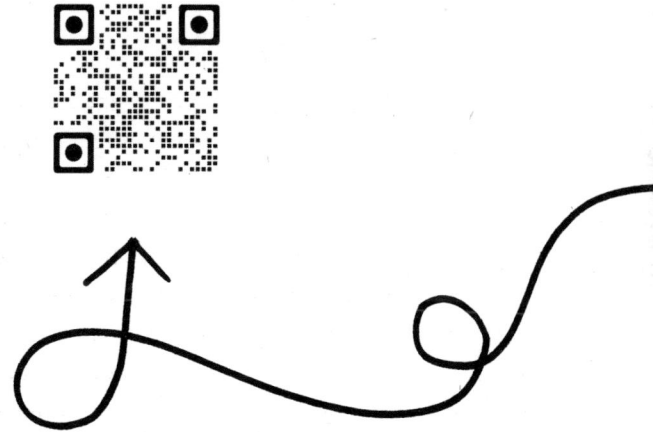

Ritual, Magic, and Intention

These confused the hell out of me at first. Once I got over my fear of the word 'ritual' *(read The Vibration of Vocabulary on page 205)*, I could really start working with magic. Ritual, through my eyes, creates a container for your magic. It's not spooky, it's a sacred pause that allows you to create space and time to set your intentions or work with magic.

So you wanna make more money? Great. Pause first, light a candle. Fill a jug with water, wrap your hands around it and charge it with the frequency of a fat-ass bank account. Feel rich and get excited that all that money is flowing effortlessly toward you. Maybe write 'CASH MONEY JUICE!' on a piece of tape and stick it to the jug. Take a deep breath, exhale. Put out your candle. Then drink your money juice every day.

Congratulations, you just cast your first spell.

Rule #1 This whole process should be uniquely your own. Whatever elements you use, choose them intentionally and give them meaning. It's more important that it means something to you than it does to anyone else. Choose what feels right. Trust yourself.

Cheat Sheet

1. **Intention = your why.** Why are you doing this and what are you doing? You wanted more money so you're making Cash Money Juice.

2. **The ritual = your action.** What did you do? In this case, you turned water into money juice (Jesus would be so proud). The pause, the candles, the jug, the water – that's the ritual; it's the practice of putting that intention into action.

3. **Magic = momentum.** How do you build a charge? You wrapped your hands around that jug and enchanted the water with frequency of a fat-ass bank account – you created a stream of energy and programmed the water. Magic is what fuels your intention forward and brings the result back. Magic amplifies the energy. Without magic, your intention is just a thought.

You can strengthen your magic by working with other elements; I love herbs, crystals, offerings, and fire (use it safely, of course – don't burn your fucking house down). Offerings are not only about reciprocity (leaving out fruits to show gratitude), they also ensure your own life force energy, body, and nervous system are not fueling the manifestation. Flowers, rice, or whatever you offer, provides life force, vitality, and support. These offerings help power and drive your intentions forward. They gas up your magic, so you don't have to. The energy needs to come from somewhere; you don't have to sacrifice your own. Crystals hold specific frequencies that can enhance your work as well. Herbs, both dried and fresh, can be used in the same way. The catch? They're all subordinate to humans – not in an egoic way, but they require direction. You must command them.

Tell them how to work for you. With love and gratitude, of course. I said command, not demand. Don't be a bitch. They are here to be in service to us, but that service needs a gentle direction.

For my Wizards, Witches, & Warlocks!

Creating *Your* Practice

Practice over perfection.

We don't practice to perfect things, we practice to *perceive* things. When we create an intentional moment (ideally in the morning) we set the tone for our day. We clear our head and our energy field, and we create distance between us and the world. Creating space creates choice. This is the process of co-creation. Without it, we're on autopilot – moving forward without understanding what we're building or why.

Your practice is your anchor, helping you ground into a calmer experience when the storms roll in. Maybe it's your naggy mother-in-law, or Janice from accounting, chasin' you down for your fucking expenses. Maybe your kid is actually kind of annoying and you don't wanna snap at them because your dad always snapped at you and now you're reading this book trying to heal your daddy issues. Practices help us avoid damaging ourselves and other people. Clearing and protecting your energy should be an ongoing practice *(see page 168)*. Like cleaning your house, you don't mop it once and you're done forever. It never ends. I take salt baths or dip in the ocean. Sometimes I cry in the privacy of my little hatchback Mercedes (this one is more of an impromptu practice, but a practice nonetheless).

Practice is both a verb and a noun. We have to actualize it, embody it. We're looking for momentum over miracles. Doing something consistently builds energy. It takes time to build your practice, but you'll notice when it's starting to work. You'll honk less, bitch less, and roll your eyes less. You'll have more compassion for yourself and others, and like everything else, when you commit to something there's a compounding effect. Micro-adjustments add up to major change over time and even 1 percent every day shifts a lot along the way.

Consistency builds self-trust. Show up, every day, as best you can. Sometimes you only have 20 percent to give – give that. This is an experiment, not an exam, so don't take it too seriously. But practice whenever you can. Even when it's messy and imperfect. It's a practice, not a performance.

Perfect your practice, don't practice for perfection.

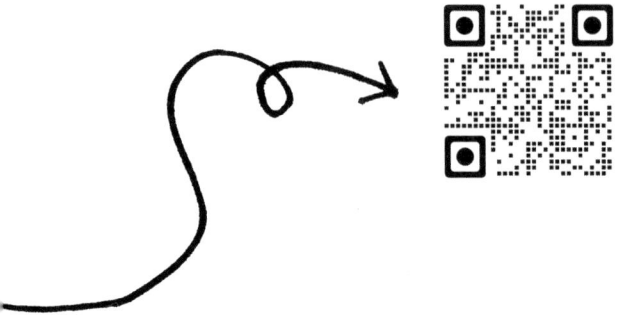

Digestion
(See, Hear, Eat, Do)

What's nourishing you at any given moment? I'm not just talking about food and I'm not gonna shame you for having more garlic bread. Nourishment is about everything that fuels us.

 Everything has a frequency. Food. Conversations. Music. Instagram. Websites. People. Everything. When we listen to certain music, it influences our energy. So do books, like the one you're reading. Is it a helpful influence? I hope so, it took a long-ass time to write it. It has a unique frequency, a force to it, just like your food, your best friend, and your favorite movie. This is why it's important to ask yourself, *How does this impact me and why do I consume it?*

Your system (mentally, physically, emotionally, and energetically) can only take so much stimulation. If we're constantly eating, our bodies malfunction. We get sick. We need to metabolize what's been consumed before reaching for more. The same happens with your mind and emotions. If you're mentally or emotionally overstimulated without time to rest, you enter a state of survival. There's too much to process; it's all backed up. You're constipated. All that gas and nowhere to go? Painful. We need to fully digest before consuming more. You need to fart, babe. We need down time. Without digestion, we get overwhelmed, resentful, or worse: we burn ourselves out.

When you're on screens all day, bombarded with information and notifications, your nervous system is constantly consuming. We can become dysregulated and overwhelmed. I fall into this trap weekly.

Even with healing we over-consume. Sometimes I force myself to take 'time off' from trying to fix things about myself. Especially if I'm getting too serious about it. If we're constantly working on ourselves without accepting who we are, we've lost the fucking plot.

Go enjoy your life. You're not a science fair project.

This is an experiment, have fun with it. Find somethin' you like – try it out for a bit, then maybe add something else. If you don't like something, stop. But don't lose your fuckin' mind trying to apply 300 pages of new ideas at once. Don't do it. Pick a few and play. Digest, metabolize it, then play some more. Don't overdo it.

When overconsumption becomes abusive, maybe it's drinking or weed, the consciousness of that thing seeks correction and begins to push back on us. It creates friction, discomfort, chaos, maybe even disease.

Consciousness seeks harmony.

Without harmony, it can become destructive.

Michelle, my friend who runs The Auric Life, blew my mind when she asked me if marijuana was a man, and my friend was dating him, and the relationship between the two of them was the same relationship I have with smoking weed, *would I consider it healthy or toxic?*

My answer at that time was toxic.

She explained to me how when you abuse something it naturally returns that abuse – just like a toxic relationship. It matches your vibration.

When you're conscious and in harmony with something, the energy returns as harmony. When you're abusing something, it returns as abuse.

★ So, what are you consuming and how much of it?

Don't beat yourself up if you don't like what you see, just pivot if you need to. I want you to consider what's really fueling you, and I'm not just talking about food.

There's some food for thought.

Consumption vs. Creation

Have you ever scrolled on your phone for like three straight hours and felt your brain rot? No? Just me? Maybe you watched an entire Netflix series in 48 hours? Just me again? You ever put 18 items in your online shopping cart then buy nothing? Or call four friends to get advice, then act on none of it? Maybe you just sit there snacking all night, mindlessly consuming whatever is in front of you. Another podcast. Another self-help book. Another event. Another drink. Another coffee, cigarette, joint, another fuck, ok... enough.

Overconsumption keeps you in a slump. A bit of a depressive state. Slow, sluggish, mundane. Don't get me wrong, we should be able to couch-potato once in a while, but too much tater tot ain't hot. Too much consumption numbs us out. Constant information puts us in a state of freeze. Hypnotized. Binging just feeds the void. It breeds stagnation and we leak energy and vitality when we're constantly consuming (*read Digestion on page 237*).

The world needs you to create and contribute your magic. I'm gonna get a bit woo-woo here and say that the 'powers that be' want you to stay stuck on your couch consuming Netflix, and Twitter, and Uber Eats all day. There's a tug of war for your attention. Consumption is addictive and it's stealing your capacity to feel, create, and know yourself.

The antidote is creation.

Creation channels our emotions into something real. It sparks inspiration and awe. Creative movement wakes up the parts of us that lie dormant. Creativity energizes, inspires, and awakens us to ourselves, our gifts, our community, and our Dharma *(read about Dharma on page 213)*. It connects us with our purpose and invites play. If you find yourself disappearing into a depressive digital void, go create something. Anything. It'll wake you back up.

That doesn't mean you can't roll a fat blunt and eat a big slice of cake while watching reruns of Tyra Banks' psychological warfare experiment *America's Next Top Model*, but we might need some boundaries.

Take a break from the TV.

Go paint something.

Sing.

Dance.

IDGAF what you create, just create something. *I'M ROOTING FOR YOU!*

Arts and Creativity

If you haven't read Consumption vs. Creation (*see page 240)*, then bounce over there and then come back to this one.

Not only do I want to selfishly plug my own music, art, and creativity (yes, I'm also a poet, a popstar, and a pirate learning violin, no big deal...) but I wanted to touch on the importance of arts and creativity for all of us. Whether you're feeling stuck or a bit directionless or everything's fine and you're ready to expand again, art and creativity is your golden ticket. Why? Here's why:

1. **Self-discovery and emotional processing:** Creating something reveals the forces that are moving in the shadows, it helps bring forward suppressed feelings, and it allows us to access parts of ourselves that we can't access with logic. When we're feeling something, but don't know what (or maybe we do know), we can create something to move the energy and integrate the experience.

2. **Increased problem-solving skills:** When we create things we begin to think more creatively, the process naturally enhances our ability to feel into multiple solutions and approach things from new angles.

3. **Heightened intuition:** Bypassing our logical mind allows us to feel into what's right and wrong. Creativity strengthens our ability to trust ourselves and our inner guidance.

4. **Community contribution:** Art sparks dialogue, helps shape culture, and allows you to contribute something unique – something only you can create.

5. **Maybe you're Beyoncé**

'Okay, Chris... but I'm not an artist.'

THE FUCK YOU'RE NOT.

Shut up and paint.

Let's get Artsy Fartsy

Using Esoteric Tools

There are so many tools to choose from to help focus your energy and intent. Whether you're connecting to Source or co-creating your reality, you'll find that at different times you connect with different tools, practices, and people. That's normal. This is about you and what makes sense to you, and what keeps you curious and feeling supported. Experiment with some of these tools and see what resonates. Literally go out and buy a deck of cards, or runes, or whatever tickles your pickle, and dedicate some time, every day, to connect with it. If you already have a favorite tool, maybe try one more. My mentor told me there's no point in having 100 tools you're mediocre with when you can have two you're really good at, and I agree. I love tarot and astrology, and I like working with magic (the elements, candles, etc.). Those are my favorite tools, but I sometimes dabble in runes and other things. Here are some other tools to play with.

Pick one and try it out.

Depending on what you're doing, your tools might change, that's fine. As you work with them over time your ability to intuit, and their power, will increase dramatically.

Some Helpful Tools

- **Tarot** (obviously, this is my #1) – A guide for understanding the energetic dynamics of yourself, other people, relationships, opportunities, etc.

- **Astrology** – If you don't understand the language of astrology, I would highly recommend learning it (it's incredibly useful!)

- **Tuning Forks/Singing Bowls** – Vibrational tools to balance and align energy

- **Incense/Resin/Herbs** – Shifts vibration, opens rituals, supports focus, and activates specific energies and intentions

- **Pendulum/Dowsing Rods** – Used for inquiry, identifying where energy is located, and if there's balance or not

- **Crystal Ball/Coffee Grinds/Tea Leaves** – Intuitive readings (like tarot) that help to understand the energetics of a person or event; great for predictions (I LOVE reading espresso cups!)

- **Magic Wand/Staff** – Great for directing energy, intention, and ritual

Activating Abundance

I noticed in Portugal when you're paying by card, they almost always skip over the option to tip. Unless you have cash, you can't leave them a thing. They cancel the tip on themselves. How can you receive anything if you're not setting yourself up to receive it?

Where do you cancel the tip on yourself?

Where are you not giving people the option to support you?

Do you turn down help?

Are you afraid to ask?

Do you brush away compliments?

Are you slow to raise your hand even though you know the answer?

Do you stand in the back of the dance class when you really wanna shake that thang?

So, is it you? Are you blocking your own blessings?

We all want more from life, but more means something different to all of us. Heed my warning: Define what type of abundance you want before you start calling it in. Abundance isn't just rooted in pleasure – we can manifest abundance of pain, or problems, or debt, it just depends on how you're working with the energy. The planet Jupiter rules abundance, and Jupiter expands everything. The good and the bad. Jupiter needs guardrails – Jupiter needs Saturn. This isn't a lesson on astrology but Saturn invites boundaries and limits. Sometimes we think he's just being an asshole when in reality he's asking us to choose a fucking direction, and stick with it. What is it that you want to grow, and why? What's your goal? Great. Set it, then set up guardrails, and expand in that specific direction.

Abundance for you might look like a Gucci t-shirt for your dog or having way more free time. You'll only really know what's important to you once you've connected deeper with yourself on a soul level. Alignment invites opportunity. Alignment is your cash cow. We dig into this deeper on the QR codes but true alignment stems from our inner child. When we're in play, awe, and wonder, we easily drop into a flow state. This is when we get lost in moment, having fun, laughing, forgetting where we are or what time it is. This is where you want to be, energetically. This flow state invites discovery, which leads to purpose. Our purpose leads us to service, or our Dharma *(read about this on page 214)*. And the combination of this will align you with opportunities like never before.

This is how we truly activate abundance. Not through hustle culture, through finding our flow.

When you begin to pour money into the world around you, directing it toward those who need it most, you really crack the code. When money flows out from you in meaningful ways then everything gets amplified, but you need to do it with a pure heart.

Where would you like to provide support?

In what ways would you like to pour into your community? *give back*

Just don't fall into martyrdom and give it all away – keep some for yourself too, babe. There's a reason you're the one receiving it. Use it to keep yourself strong and healthy – the better you are, the better those around you are. You have to meet your own needs first. Fill your own cup, so that you're taken care of and can be a clean channel for abundance to flow through. It's not going to flow through some dirty ass pot. You gotta be a gorgeous Ace of Cups!

So, define abundance, set some goals, create some boundaries and take care of yourself. Pour only from a cup that runneth over.

More Joy, More Play

Joy is love in motion. Play is the embodiment of joy. Together, these two powerful states of being can shift things, create opportunities, and inspire change. Joy is infectious. It spreads. In the best way possible, it's contagious. It allows us to access our highest expression. It taps us into creativity and authenticity, and everything good stems from there. Without joy we're rigid, resentful; over time, this calcifies and becomes a personality trait. We all know a grumpy Gus somewhere and we know it's not the vibe. You can literally see it on their face. It's like their mood melted into their features and never left. Our truth is rooted in play, our abundance is rooted in play, all our fuckin' fun is rooted in play, and this is where your highest timeline will manifest. Intentionally co-creating your reality is a creative process and creativity is playful. Joy and play are essential to our design.

It took me a long time to realize that I avoid joy for the fear of losing it. I was a super fun, creative, expressive child, until I wasn't. Bullying, traumas, family bullshit, not to mention society psychologically beating me down into a state of submission – at some point I lost my spark. I realized it wasn't safe to express myself fully or to live in a constant state of play. Joy felt like it jeopardized my safety. In many ways, once upon a time, it did. But as we grow, we can create safe spaces for ourselves. We can return to play. Joy is activism in this day and age. We're wired to compete and compare and this is the antithesis to joy. We're scared of being seen, and vulnerable, and judged, and this is the enemy of play. Society, religion, structures, even family and friends, have both consciously and unconsciously created control mechanisms to limit our joy. We think if we stay small, we stay safe. If we limit joy, we limit risk. In reality, it limits us from experiencing what makes us feel most alive.

And you thought the zombie apocalypse was just a Hollywood movie.

There are so many reasons we shut ourselves down. Trauma responses contribute to hyper-vigilance. Living in fight or flight means our nervous system is conditioned to remain on edge, like we're always on guard. Joy and play require safety, relaxation, and space. If we're stuck in the rat race or always consuming fearful media, it's hard to find space to play. It's hard to find our drive. Fear weakens our energy field, it dampens our experiences, and it robs us of expansion. Many of us avoid joy out of fear of losing it – like if we feel it fully it may be ripped away, so we numb ourselves to it or we sabotage things before they can invite joy in. We replay mistakes or get caught in shame or loops of guilt and we convince ourselves that we don't deserve it. Some of us carry a lot of punishment programming from religion, our ancestors, or other structures that make us think we must earn joy. It's not something we can just have; we have to work for it. We have to struggle for it. So many of us only find joy in the celebration of the strife it took to get there, wearing our struggle like a badge of honor. I love you, but this is all fucking bullshit. We need to get away from these ideologies. We need to carve out space for play. And we don't need to work for it.

We don't need to chase the highs of extreme pleasure, we can work micro-moments of joy into our day. Stop and smell the roses. Literally. I do it and every time I smell a flower I fucking love it. How could you not? That beautiful thing has a beautiful smell? It's kinda fuckin' wild, no? If you don't think so then we need to strengthen your sense of awe and wonder. Twirl. Spin. Dance in the morning, even just to one song. I know it sounds simple and maybe even stupid, but trust me, it shifts things over time.

Choose a comedy instead of your weird little murder mystery. Before bed every night I acknowledge ten things I'm grateful for from that day and I sit with a smirk on my face and love in my heart and I intentionally feel a moment of joy and laughter. We need to reawaken this part of ourselves. It's still there, I promise. It's just buried under some bullshit that's not even yours. So, experiment with what makes you feel happy. Experiment with play, especially as an adult. Have the audacity to roll down a fucking hill just for the fun of it (my best friend Anna loves this shit; she gets branches in her hair and everything). I promise you, slowly but surely, when you activate joy and play in your life again, intentionally carving out time for it, new doors will open and the Universe will meet you with miracles. Try it out.

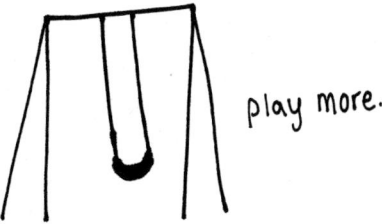

play more.

The Audacity to Be
Soft Yet Bold

Not all words equal wisdom. More volume does not equal more power. We've been taught to obey authority, the ones who rule with an iron fist, but dominance is rooted in fear, insecurity, and lack of true power. True power is soft and direct. Honest, yet bold. Bold is inspiring, dominance is intimidating. I've noticed the loudest person in the room is typically the weakest or most fragile, and aggression is often rooted in fear of their weaknesses being revealed.

When we're truly rooted in our power there's no need for drama or dominance. We direct energy much better when it comes from a calm, grounded state. Centered and steady, clear and concise. When we're anchored in our truth, we can share it confidently, and there's no need to raise our voice. Anger masks vulnerability and creates an outward energetic explosion; it's reactive, unstable, and scattered. It fragments us and keeps us shattered in too many pieces. When we're split open, we leak energy. Power requires coherence and connection, and connection is rooted in equity and respect. When your energy is steady, not loud and chaotic, people lean in to listen. They're happy to help, and from here, you can create. This is how you work with and shape energy; through collective flow, not force.

When you know who you are you have nothing to prove.

Trust from others is the byproduct of you being anchored into your authentic self. Owning your truth allows others to own theirs. This creates real intimacy and change. Have you ever met a beautiful person and tried to force them into a relationship with you? I fucking hope not. It doesn't work like that and you're likely to get arrested

We're all looking for connection, even the angry, dominant ones. They probably need it the most, but they're going about it in all the wrong ways.

Audacity isn't only tap-dancing onto center stage with a top hat and high kicks. This type of audacity is about being soft in a world that's addicted to being hard. The audacity to be gentle when they want you to fight. To return to love and kindness. The audacity to slow things down when everything else is speeding up. Or to feel it all — to cry it out because you're so fucking frustrated. Or scream in a pillow instead of screaming at the lady in the grocery store because she bumped into your cart while managing twin boys.

Have the audacity to say no. No more.

Take a day to yourself. Take more time if you can.

Get offline.

Have the audacity to care for yourself in a world that feels like it forgot how to care.

Have the audacity to love yourself, and know yourself, so deeply, that their force will never interrupt your flow.

This is your reclamation of self.

Claim it, babe.

You deserve to.

Bending the Spoon

We are not separate from the world around us. We are connected to everything: the sky, the earth, the birds, your cutlery. I know it's easy to overlook because there's nothing seemingly invisible about stubbing your baby toe on the coffee table, but let me tell you, nail or no nail, matter is mostly empty space.

Our perception of things, and the expectations we place on them, quite literally give them form. If you can shift your perception, you can shift reality.

My friend Audra literally bent a spoon. Not with sheer strength and force, but by dropping into a meditative state. I simply share this to share what's possible – a new lens to see through. A shift in your perception. Our consciousness interacts with our physical reality and the impossible becomes possible when we begin to understand that it is all one. The way Audra described it, she and the spoon both disappeared into the space between the atoms. Sounds kinda wild, right? Well, if you were to look at any object through an electron microscope you would find that nothing is actually touching. Everything is in motion, vibrating, spinning, and orbiting within a field. There's space between the atoms. Everything is actually floating, and nothing is solid. We, too, are not solid in the way we think we are. We're also made of atoms, and atoms are 99.9999 percent empty space.

So there she went, slipping into the void, and when she created enough space, when she knew she was connected to all of it and none of it at the same time, she bent a fucking spoon. 'Like butter' might I add. And that's a direct quote.

When you stop seeing things the same way you've always seen them, you create space for possibility. When you no longer see yourself as separate from the world around you, you begin to access new levels of intuition, creation, and potential. I've never bent a spoon, but in my defence I've never tried. I did snap a plastic spoon in half once while digging into my Ben & Jerry's Cookie Dough ice cream a little too aggressively, but I don't think that technically counts.

I'm not expecting you to bend a spoon, either. At least not today, but I do think we could all benefit from this lesson. At the very least, I think we could begin to soften ourselves into a more malleable state, and go from there.

Shift your Reality

Do the Thing

While I was working on this book, I ordered a box of stuff from this guy who makes amazing jewelry and geometric, energetic, witchy things I can't explain. I found him randomly on Instagram and when I opened the package, I found a handwritten letter. He told me that at a really rough moment in his life in 2020 someone sent him my Virgo horoscope:

'Your horoscope told me to trust myself and take a chance on something new in 2020. You appeared at a particularly moldable moment. I was in the grind. No one had ever suggested that life could be anything else. After I saw your reading I quit my job, started this business, and it's literally the best thing that's ever happened to me.'

This shit makes me cry. Do you know how touching it is to know that my work made a difference in someone's life? Even if it is a bit cringe *(see page 165)*. There are people who were never told to go after their dreams. Some people were never told to make a change or try something new. I just hope that this book can be that for you. I hope you know I support you going after your dream. I went after mine and it worked out just fine. Yours could work out even better.

Your dream doesn't need to be the biggest and the loudest. It can be something simple. It can be me here typing these words to you on my orange vintage typewriter. It could be calling forward the artist inside. The one you forgot. Hidden, maybe buried. Do you want to splash paint across a canvas in a studio apartment on the Upper West Side? Or play music at midnight to a crowd in Madrid drinking sangria. Maybe recently you were arranging lilies and peonies in a vase and suddenly knew your dream was to own a flower shop. Fuck it – why not add a café inside!

This *Fuck It* energy *(see page 179)* will lead you to joy. So take a chance.

I believe in you.

I double dog
dare you to
doodle...

Record your affirmations as a voice note & listen before bedtime.

Brush your teeth w̄ the other hand.

Take a new class.

Ask for what you want.

art / music / clay

create something!

poetry / sketch / paint

Ask your Guides for a specific sign!

TRY SOMETHING NEW

Pay It Forward.

Do something you normally wouldn't. **

crystals / magic wand

Go to an esoteric shop & buy/try a new tool.

pendulum

Tarot

oracle

herbs

Take a solo date night.

Play.

Walk Backwards for 6 min./day

leave a love note somewhere.

Fly, Birdy, Fly!

Well, there it is, folks. Hopefully something for you to experiment with as you venture forward. I feel like a baby bird mama, but not the throw-up-in-your-mouth kind, the kind that's proud of you for leaving the nest. Even if you death-dive into a bush, you'll survive. Just get back up and flap those fuckin' wings.

For some of you this may be the beginning of an exciting new life – good luck, my young grasshopper. For others, you may have heard this shit before, but maybe this time it smelt a lil' different. Either way, I hope something clicks. If you do decide to come back to this book at some point, you'll read it through a new lens. The spiralic nature of your ever-expanding consciousness will provide new insights from old chapters. As time progresses, we'll update the QR Codes and do what we can to continue supporting your journey. Like you, this book, the online community, and the digital resources are ever evolving.

Ram Dass once said, 'I can do nothing for you but work on myself' and honestly lil' Rammy, mic-drop!

What you learn here can radiate out and reshape the world around you. Your contributions to the collective, both big and small, do not go unnoticed, and thank you for doing this work. You're helping us all create a better world. And I appreciate you being here.

Thank you for helping me live out my dreams. Now go live out yours.

love
you.

This book is not filled with instructions; it's an invitation to play with these ideas and make them your own. So, make them your own. Trust yourself.

And have the audacity to experiment along the way.

Thank Yous

First and foremost, I'd like to thank myself. Snoop Dogg did that once and I loved the audacity he had to put himself first. I get it – I've been by my side through thick and thin, and it has not always been easy. I've seen the darkest of days and still shown up with a smile, as best I could. I only wish I could have gone back and been there for myself even more so. Moving forward I will, because my needs matter.

I thank the Universe for gifting me such beauty and pain. The moments that shaped me into everything that led me to this exact moment. I thank Wheelhouse, my beautiful community center, for giving me a space to birth this book, and for allowing me to give back to the community, to create safety and play for myself and others.

I thank my mom for never giving up and doing whatever she could to make sure that we always had what we needed. I thank my dad for being one of my greatest teachers. I thank my siblings for journeying through this life with me; and my twin nephews for reminding me how beautiful the simple things can be. Maverick, my dog, Loki, my cat, and our new farm – thank you for helping me rewrite my story of home, and what safety and security feels like.

I thank Don, my best friend and my only mentor, for always believing in me. For teaching me not to give a fuck what other people think. For always toasting us and those like us, the damn few. For seeing in me what nobody else saw, at a time when I needed it most, and for being there through all of the darkness that cracked me open. So much of the medicine I share is the fruit from a seed you planted.

I thank Daniella for helping me hold the vision of what's possible; for standing by my side, no matter what.

I thank Crystal and Shayla for their invaluable insight. I thank Rachel and Amy for their support through this writing process and the fucking mess I made of it; to Jack for the audacious cover design; to Leanne and Becky for the hours and hours we spent on doodles and diagrams, and advocating for our childish designs; and to everyone else on the publishing team who helped bring structure to everything that flowed through me. A special thanks to Emma, my editor, I absolutely love your work.

I thank Anna for helping me dream again and for the fairy magic she brings to me and so many others.

Thank you Eduardo for hitting that spot. Thank you Lisbon and all of my game night friends. Thank you to the friends and lightworkers who support me in every which way – you know who you are. Thank you to my international community, those who have generously received and supported so much of my work. I truly thank you. I love you. This book is for all of us.

And lastly, I thank this book – an entity of its own – for trusting me with these words and allowing me to steward through this conversation to help others. Thank you for peeling back the layers of what no longer is, so I could become who I was meant to be through the process of writing you and rewilding myself. Thank you. Thank you. Thank you.

Thank you! xo

Me

About the Author

Chris Corsini is a psychic, intuitive energy worker, and tarot card reader whose astrology and moon-cycle workshops have inspired a global community to live with greater awareness and authenticity. His dynamic, down-to-earth style and 'freakishly accurate' readings have made him a trusted guide for everyone from A-list celebrities to spiritual newcomers.

After years working as a certified ASL/English interpreter, Chris realized the need for greater inclusivity in wellness spaces and built a community that aims to make everyone feel seen and supported. A passionate advocate for accessibility, he does what he can to support charitable causes, including those supporting Deaf and Disabled populations, LGBTQIA2S+, minority racial and ethnic groups, and Indigenous communities.

Through all he does, Chris encourages others to trust their intuition, embrace change, and live with courage, compassion, and audacity.

ASL Edition

A signed version??? Correct. We had the audacity to put this book both in hands and on hands. Scan the QR code below for exclusive access to the ASL version of *The Audacity Experiment*. Yes, the whole thing, signed by yours truly. Enjoy.

if you want to make your content accessible also, Scan here to Explore How!

We hope you enjoyed this Hay House book. If you'd like to receive our online catalogue featuring additional information on Hay House books and products, please contact:

Hay House UK Ltd
1st Floor, Crawford Corner,
91–93 Baker Street, London W1U 6QQ
Tel: +44 (0)20 3927 7290; www.hayhouse.co.uk

———

Published in the United States of America by:
Hay House LLC
PO Box 5100, Carlsbad, CA 92018-5100
Tel: (760) 431-7695 or (800) 654-5126
www.hayhouse.com

Published in Australia by:
Hay House Australia Publishing Pty Ltd
18/36 Ralph St., Alexandria NSW 2015
Tel: +61 (02) 9669 4299
www.hayhouse.com.au

Published in India by:
Hay House Publishers (India) Pvt Ltd
Muskaan Complex, Plot No. 3,
B-2, Vasant Kunj, New Delhi 110 070
Tel: +91 11 41761620
www.hayhouse.co.in

———

Let Your Soul Grow

Experience life-changing transformation – one video
at a time – with guidance from the world's leading experts.

www.healyourlifeplus.com

CONNECT WITH
HAY HOUSE
ONLINE

🌐 hayhouse.co.uk   **f** @hayhouse

📷 @hayhouseuk   🦋 @hayhouseuk.bsky.social

♪ @hayhouseuk   ▶ @HayHousePresents

Find out all about our latest books & card decks • Be the first
to know about exclusive discounts • Interact with our authors in
live broadcasts • Celebrate the cycle of the seasons with us •
Watch free videos from your favourite authors •
Connect with like-minded souls

'The gateways to wisdom and knowledge
are always open.'

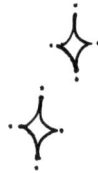

I want you to rip these out whenever you need a lil' boost of love, or magic, or *whatever*. Yes, you can redeem them at anytime. They never expire. If you haven't cracked the code yet, they're universal coupons. Kinda like the ones in America but without contributing to oil spills, deforestation, and geopolitical collapse – *allegedly* (legal said I had to tread carefully here).

Rip it out.

Charge it up.

Make sure you read the fine print.

You can keep one in your wallet or gift it to a friend. You can also make your own – it was quite easy. These ones are personally crafted just for you so I've put a lil' extra *Bippity Boppity Boo* on 'em. If you wanna get real wild, you could light one on fire* and use it in a cute lil' magic ceremony (though it will turn to ash and *it will be gone*).

Quit teasing me. Take it out already. Don't let my doodles just sit there beggin' for it. Remember at the start of this experiment when you ripped that whole fucking page out? This should be a walk in the park – it's just a strip. So, go for it.

Strip for me.

Adult supervision required.

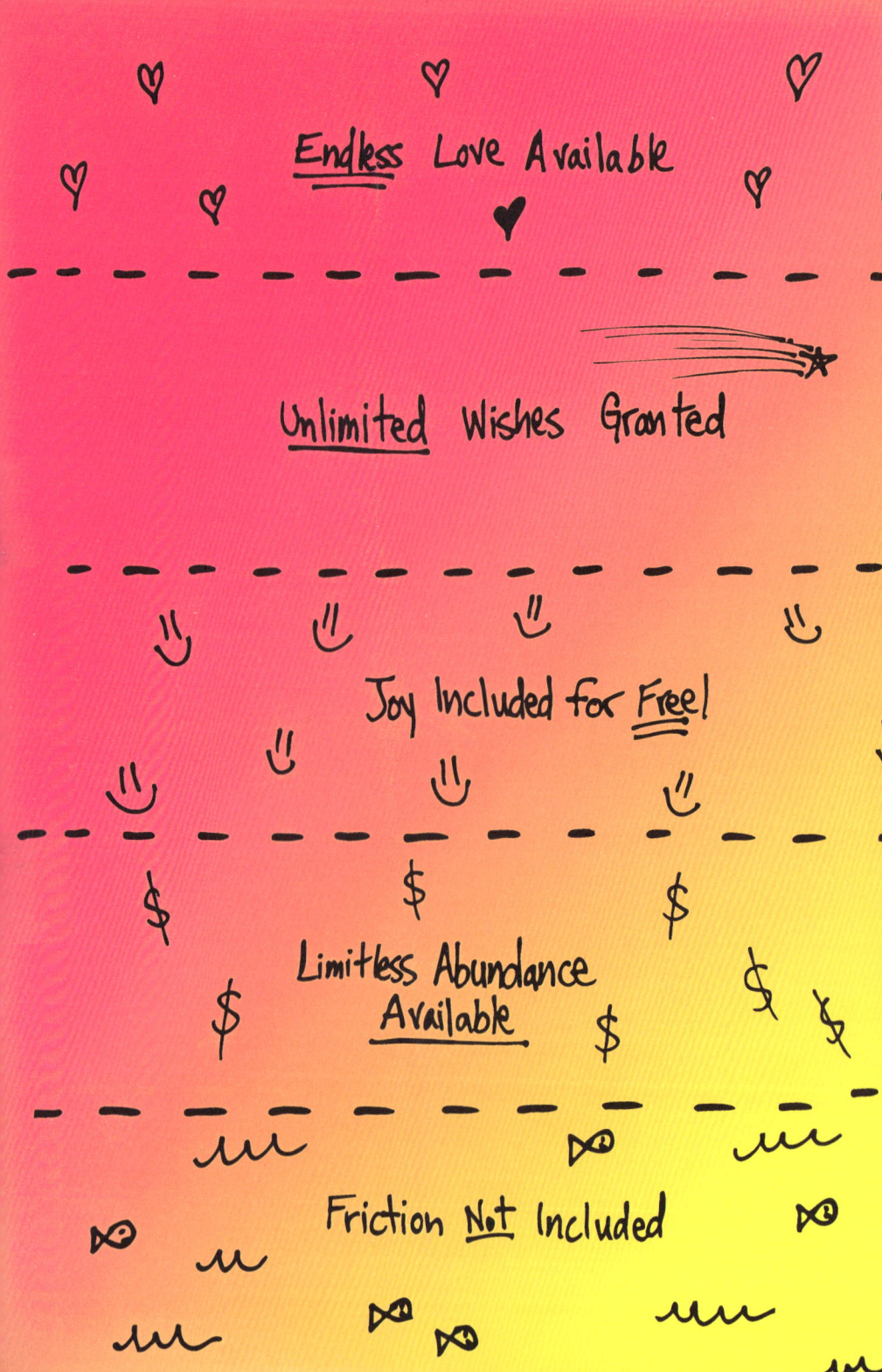